THE

KITEMAN

by

SPIKE BROWN

ILLUSTRATED BY

KARL WHITELEY

Tower Bridge Books

Tower Bridge Books

Copyright © 2024 by Spike Brown

Illustrations by Karl Whiteley

Spike Brown has asserted his right under the copyright, designs, and patents act of 1988 to be identified as the author of this book. All rights reserved.

No part of this publication may be reproduced, stored in a retrieval system, or transmitted in any form or by any means, electronic, mechanical, photocopying, recording or otherwise, without the prior permission of the copyright owner.

A catalogue record of this book is available from the British Library

For Julie & Bill, Ben & Annika

Prologue

1837 Haworth, Mr Kenyons House

The elderly gentleman, dignified features enhanced by his grizzled side whiskers, swept back mane of white hair, firm jaw denoting strictly no nonsense, humorous eyes conveying sense and wisdom, and a nose as distinguished as that of the Duke of Wellington, considered his beautiful daughter.

Steepling his fingers before the fire from the comfort of his winged armchair, he sighed heavily. "There is no change?"

"None," replied Dr Otley, studying his long-term patient kindly.

"All these lost months. My dear fellow, if only Sir James would visit once in a while, make his presence known, provide a modicum of contact, she might at least react. We have not seen him this past year, not a single letter even. Is that how a husband should behave? I know the circumstances, the accident on their honeymoon, but he seems to show scant regard. Money is sent regularly enough, I suppose."

"I hear he is a busy man. Controlling his business interests from Scrivelsby Hall. In some ways, we must not be too harsh in our views Mr Kenyon. Violet remains but a waxwork for now, a life-sized doll - the brain injury persists to debilitate her. She appears outwardly placid, unresponsive, and yet liken to yourself, I have such faith and hope that she shall one day make a full recovery. I have studied many volumes by eminent Swiss professors, experts in their field that attest there are such cases, admittedly few, where this 'stalling' of the brain proves temporary, and the patient makes a full recovery."

"I know, I know, Dr Otley. We have discussed this often." He replied solemnly, "It's a terrible dichotomy the way Sir James quit Scrivelsby Hall after such a splendid church summer wedding, departing for Lakeland in a fine white carriage to the cheers of well-wishers – train to Penrith, road to Keswick – only to return but three days later from Derwent Water. His wife blanketed on a stretcher carried by staff from a horse ambulance. We know all that – the boating accident on the lake. Whose fault? No one's. Violet slipped and knocked her head, plimsolls to blame, on a slippery deck. Dear Lord, I ponder the circumstances over and over. Is it at all probable that Sir James bares guilt - feels himself somehow responsible? I know not. Confound the fellow, surely his beholden duty is to his wife. Miss Leyden ..." he called out to his housekeeper, who cared for his daughter. "Take Violet for her morning ride, could you? And might you deliver a note to my dear friend, the Rev Patrick Brontë, up at the parsonage while you're about it."

The housekeeper began to make ready the wheeled contraption in the hall. The bath chair, despite the steep hills, being the best form of mobility outdoors.

Dr Otley had always considered Violet Kenyon the loveliest person alive. As a young boy, he had admired her from afar, and now himself a tall and swarthy gentleman of two-and-thirty years, he remained devoted to her care, marvelling at her cruel fate.

How the boating injury left not a single scar or blemish upon her physical self, a single blow to the front of the head robbing her of her short and long-term memory - the ability to appreciate her own personality, her beauty. She was at least not bedridden, and was able to move and eat with assistance, but remained but waxwork of herself, personality imprisoned. How he hoped and prayed her life would one day flourish again and she should be allowed to see the light of normality.

One

Gordon Aboyne was an intense young man, an acquaintance of the Brontë's, who had taken a shine to Charlotte, the eldest sibling.

He enjoyed basking in the sister's creative enthusiasm while they wrote and painted round the dining room table. Mr Aboyne was not without eccentricity, which appealed to the Brontës, although the father, Patrick, remained aloof, wary of the more and more frequent visitor to their house on top of the hill.

Attired in a shiny black suit and creaking, elastic-sided boots, Aboyne laid open his large portfolio folder and withdrew a sheaf of drawings for the girl's perusal.

"You are of a morbid turn?" Enquired Emily, making a brief but serious study.

"No, not at all. The subject interests me," he answered, fiddling with his frayed cuff.

"But you nonetheless 'haunt'." Charlotte attempted a weak smile, a glance between sisters, barely able to conceal their giggles. "Forgive me, sir, that is the improper expression. You surely must spend considerable time in such places."

"If you say so."

"The sketches are well executed and show a flair for your subject," said Anne. "If funerals and mortuary monuments are your specialism, I wonder whether there's a career as a cemetery artist to be had out of this. They are not without merit. Have you sold any of these images, approached a periodical, submitted to a publisher?"

"You're very kind," he replied bluntly. "Alas, nothing to talk of."

Charlotte, the eldest, provided a helpful suggestion. "Would it not be better to concentrate your abilities less along Gothic lines, more upon homely subjects popular in the public mind? Cottage scenes, family pets, city architecture, the craggy moorland landscape of the Pennines which we ourselves draw so much inspiration."

"Graveyards and cemeteries, however varied the location, I just can't see this sort of thing catching on with galleries and publications," said Anne.

"Who knows?" sighed Emily. "One day, the etiquette of mourning may become immensely fashionable, an affair of the masses, emporiums in Harrogate and York displaying funerary departments. Gordon Aboyne may become a household name. Before long, his graveside scenes reproduced on Isaiah Wedgwood's jugs, soup tureens, plates, branching out into wallpaper prints, curtains even, a trend to be embraced wholeheartedly by the Queen herself."

The visitor bowed gracefully, aware that gentle teasing was taking place amongst the sisterhood, yet he respected their creative genius and was not the slightest bit put out. Emily's throwaway suggestion of wallpaper printed with his graves and monuments, hearse and mourning coaches set his head racing. "Branwell I hear was drunk again last night at the Black Bull, braying to his cronies, casting disparaging remarks about that Kenyon woman, until someone threatened to put a glass down his throat."

"Our brother is an insensitive oaf. A job on the railways working as a booking clerk, did not improve his stroppy, loud-mouthed tendencies. He was sacked and returned to the fold last week."

"Papa sees only the good and remains patient for his errant only son."

"But he drinks so much. What on earth created such a vacuous hole in his life? He is only a young fellow, about my age. A woman, I suspect," exclaimed Mr Aboyne, smoking his pipe reflectively. "Damn my eyes if it's not female mischief."

"There be no excuse to drink yourself to death," said Charlotte heatedly. "Woman or no. He is so unfair and stubborn; his outbursts make us shudder. Papa is worried he will end up entwined in a police matter, up before the Justice of the Peace then imprisoned. Or set fire to his own bed as inebriates are so often prone to do."

"Very likely," declared Anne.

The vicar, Rev Patrick Brontë like Dr Otley, was a well-regarded character. Approachable and charitable. Often seen out walking briskly round the parish doing his Christian duty. The note that he had received from Mr Kenyon touched him deeply.

The dining room door opened and, much to the sister's delight, their father poked his head round. Directing his voice firstly at the wild-haired, shabbily dressed young man smoking a churchwarden pipe, "Gordon, would you care to join my daughters and I to pray in my study. I received a note from my friend, Mr Kenyon, the fulsome architect of our new schoolhouse. Charlotte, Emily, Anne, I beseech you, devote a short time to reflection, meditation. His daughter Violet's condition is as before. Her brain remains paralysed, a tragic case indeed. Emily, a suitable hymn played upon the upright cabinet piano in my study would go down well."

"I rarely attend church, padre," replied Gordon.

"No matter, at least you're no strict Calvinist, or ranting Baptist my boy. You are most welcome. Not physically disabled, mark you, Violet is burdened by an ill-sparking brain. The cranial organ is so little understood by modern science. Startling to think that in an age of steam locomotives, piston pumps and belt-driven looms we know so little. All of you good people come to my study at once, we shall commence prayers."

And so, that they did.

Two

The following morning, the sky above windswept moorland behind Glebe House gusty and overcast, a most talked-about incident took place over at the church, taking everybody utterly by surprise.

Little Amy Clough, the parlour maid, was first to raise the alarm, followed by Tabitha, the elderly servant.

"Vicar, oh do come at once. Summat dreadful's happened. Dear o' Lor'. Someone's set to die in't graveyard, of all places."

At first, certain locals deemed the desperate individual most likely to be Branwell Brontë, dissipated son of the parson, recently sacked from the railways, about to sling himself off the church tower – a failure to his father, a victim of the drink, beaten down by baser passions, wishing to end it all. A final desperate gesture to be noticed, to find fame as his talented sisters were surely about to.

Yet, as events unfolded, it appeared not to be him at all teetering precariously upon the edge of the church tower, but rather a crazed woman wearing a bridal gown and veil.

Fussed over by Tabitha Aykroyd, without delay, gathering their capes and bonnets, for the weather was chill and autumnal that early morning, the sisters followed their energetic father, down the path, eager to ascertain the exact nature of the emergency.

Beyond the walled garden, with its lawn and borders, lay green, mossy tabletop tombs packed in with headstones jostling for space

— a crowded churchyard if ever there was one.

Bounding great strides, guided by his sexton John Brown, Rev Brontë soon saw a wildly swaying figure silhouetted against the stormy sky.

His wan, pinched face peering skywards, he shouted boldly: "Peace, my child. Pray, act not so hastily. Allow pause for your better judgement to prevail." The wind blowing about the skirts of his cassock, bowled off his clerical hat, sending it scuttling across the graves. "Whatever your problem, it is nothing a pot of tea and sober reflection on one's predicament cannot cure. Jumping from that great height solves nothing."

No reply was heard above the buffeting gusts, the gyrating figure waving her arms madly about on the summit of the bell tower, set upon her own destruction, not to be thwarted, even by a man of the cloth.

A gasp came from those witnessing the tragedy, as the woman fell forwards and took final flight, plunging rapidly, slowed only briefly by her billowing gown caught by the wind. A sickening crackle as the fluttering heap smashed headfirst into a clutch of damp, green headstones some distance from the path. The broken body travelled on for some short time, twisting round, and round before coming to rest upon a mound of claggy clay, a recently filled-in grave yet allotted no cross.

'Let her die, at least, and not linger painfully with appalling injuries', was the general view upheld by those assembled, but who could have survived such a fall anyhow?

"Stay your ground, my dears," commanded the father, cautioning his three daughters to come no further, for the shattered body would be ugly to behold. "Go back to the house, employ yourselves diligently. There is nothing more to see. Mr Brown, Mr Todge," he cried above the wind, "we must sheet the woman in all haste. Dr Otley should be summoned at once. This, the eighth of October, before nine of the clock, is destined to go down as infamous in the parish records, a black mark for St Michael's. A suicide, no less. Someone killing themselves in our own churchyard."

"By 'eck, your worship," one official answered, leaning over the destroyed remains. The burly sexton, John Brown, and assistant gravedigger, Mr Todge, first to view the carnage, huddled in their coats against the furious gusts. "Now tha's a disgrace, is that, causing us all near apoplexy. What on earth do we 'ave 'ere?"

Fig 1

Three

The day had been long with visits to many patients. Ensconced in Mr Kenyon's sitting room, lulled by the crackling coals in the grate and steady tick-tock of the grandfather clock in the hall, Dr Otley welcome as a son in the architect's home, was more than content to keep company with Violet sat in her armchair opposite.

At some stage he had nodded off. When he last looked up from his book, she had been staring into space, hands folded primly on her lap. The casement clock in the hall struck the quarter hour. Mr Kenyon was himself upstairs in his study busy at his drawing board, the servants employed in the kitchen creating a fine supper.

Whilst in the midst of some tepid imaginings of an ill-formed dream, part in this world, part in another, his chin slumped upon his chest, his copy of the *Lancet* fallen onto the carpet, he heard a charming, erudite, feminine voice breaking through his muddy consciousness.

"My dearest Samuel, how long have you watched over me?"

He correspondingly felt icy-cold fingers tenderly encircling his wrist and awoke, to find the face of Violet Kenyon staring into his own, having quit her chair. The doctor's reaction, perfectly understandable given the circumstances. Violet's physiognomy had, for nearly a year now, been more akin to a shop window mannequin, else a subject of a waxwork. He screamed his head off!

Causing Mr Kenyon, on the floor above, to abandon his parabolic design for a new assembly room, quit his oak-panelled study and go thumping downstairs to see what was happening. Likewise, causing Mrs Leyden, the housekeeper, cook also, to leave the kitchen, both bursting in upon the fireside proceedings.

How quickly anxious expressions turned to ones of joy when the reality of the situation dawned – a deliriously content Violet Kenyon knelt at the feet of Dr Otley, clasping his hand in hers, surprisingly returned to normality. Her brain functions restored, mistress of the house once more, comfortable, healthy and happy.

A change had taken place in their mistress – her personality restored – which offset the doctor's initial shock and disbelief.

Soon the little group settled into hilarity, laughter and affectionate hugs.

Although a more sombre issue was raised unexpectedly at the supper table over lamb cutlets later that night.

"My dear Violet," said Mr Kenyon, overwhelmed by euphoria at his daughter being alive and zestful for the first time in ages, "we must contact Sir James Grueldyke without delay," he enthused over his meal. "I am sure he shall be heartily glad of your sudden recovery, your speech restored. You are the personable, affectionate young lady I remember at the wedding. My own sweet-natured, sensitive, lovely daughter returned to the fold. Oh, if your mother were still alive, what would she say if she were amongst us now? Dr Otley, charge your glass, sir, a celebration is in order. I must inform everyone. My friend Patrick Brontë shall be delighted. I shall compose a letter to Sir James at Scrivelsby Hall and send a rider without further ado. Barton can saddle a horse and make haste across the moors."

The composed and happy expression on Violet's face clouded over. "If I ever see Sir James again, I swear I might be inclined to kill him, to strike him dead," said she with such intensity it warped the room's atmosphere. Her features softening when she beheld Dr Otley's admiring gaze, he saw this outburst as proof of a returning strength of mind and will. "Forgive my ardour, but I soundly believe, while I have been sick in mind, grandfather's fortune, legally mine, shall have become much depleted. What does the law tell us, Papa?"

"Well, naturally, on marriage, your husband took control - custodial and property rights - but in reality, you should have had a say in how the money was spent."

"Had I been able to seek the advice of our family lawyer 'Old Hawley', I should have explained how my husband attempted to murder me on my honeymoon. It was never an accident." She broke into sobs. Dr Otley rushed to her side, taking her frail, delicate hand in his. "That beast, that vile man tried to forcibly push me off the sailboat so that I might drown. Failing this, during the struggle, my head struck against the tiller and his purpose was achieved anyhow. I remember his outrage, on the part of my husband, as though it happened only yesterday. My recall of events is completely vivid. At Keswick, we stayed at the Royal Oak Hotel. Guides, boats and ponies were easily enough hired from the inn, and for the following morning, my husband arranged that he and I should go sailing upon Derwent Water in sight of the mountains of Borrowdale. He assured me he was himself expert and that the small sailing craft was ideal for two persons. It was on this long body of water that this all took place."

Mr Kenyon, the architect, looked doubtful, taking his daughter's pronouncement with a pinch of salt, wondering perhaps whether she was exaggerating. Sir James had always struck him as a decent sort: thrifty, careful with his money, certainly. Alas, his infamous forebears commemorated in oil paintings at Scrivelsby Hall, were, for the most part, debauched earls addicted to gambling, drink, and wenches.

"My poor child, this is not like you, Violet. What cares our present company for money, for financial concerns, when your health has been so miraculously restored. Talk of killing Sir James is so unladylike. You appear much agitated. Come, come, daughter of mine, if you persist in worrying over money, I shall, of course, summon Old Hawley, the family solicitor, in the morning. You had better air your grievances against your husband privately. For your own sake, not a word of this must reach Sir James Grueldyke's ears."

The father was aware that while he had been talking, Dr Samuel Otley and his vivacious daughter had eyes only for each other. A bond more than simple friendship was swiftly developing. Dammit, they were clearly in love. What might unfold in the future? She was a married woman, after all.

Four

Familiar to a certain visitor to Haworth parsonage upon a rainy Wednesday afternoon in October was the polished pedestal table central to the dining room where presently Emily's mahogany artist's box lay open.

Here in this room at Glebe House was the hub of numerous projects consistently on the boil.

The table's surface littered with novels (written in small handwriting), poetry, sketches, water colours: the talent these ladies possessed, their prolific endeavours, inevitably attracted Mr Aboyne or 'the cemetery artist' as he had been nicknamed, to attend upon the Brontë sisters to share their pleasant banter, to witness their works in progress, but most importantly, to seek the company of Charlotte, with whom he was particularly fond.

Granted, Gordon was able to follow his own artistic endeavours due to an aunt's generous legacy, which, although by no means wealthy, allowed him to be independent and free from the drudge of the labour market. Able to indulge his passion for committing to paper by means of pencil and charcoal, images of mortuary monuments, vaults, funeral cortèges, mourners stood around the grave and all else associated with Yorkshire graveyards and cemeteries.

"Who was it, I wonder," questioned Charlotte, scratching the ears of Emily's bristling mastiff *Keeper*, who had deserted his mistress, curling his considerable shaggy bulk instead beside her own chair, "went to the bother of dressing up a scarecrow in a bridal gown and veil. I mean, the audacity, the heartlessness of presenting a suicidal leap from the top of the church tower to a group of parishioners below. In of all places, a sacred place of internment, a graveyard."

"But to control such a kite, lest we forget, the sheer skill required to sail the bride atop of the church tower in the first place, let alone hold her steady on the parapet," gushed Anne, passing a plate of biscuits to Gordon. "To fly a kite of such elaborate construction, we were perceptively duped, utterly fooled. Honestly, Mr Aboyne, the dramatic quality of the incident. Our very own short-sighted Papa pleaded for this turnip-headed bride to come down."

"And down she came, with a crunching crackle of wood," Emily laughed.

"The scarecrow bride will be famous all over Yorkshire. The newspapers shall proclaim her tragedy far and wide. The journalistic hacks of the *Halifax Guardian*, *The Yorkshire Post*, spout forth upon her notoriety."

"Her wedding regalia, her gown, her veil fettered to wooden struts that she might inflate, become airborne."

"Utilising the strong gusts, this kite flyer, must have jerked the strings free, thus she fell to the ground."

"First to witness the shattered kite frame, torn garments, the bridal veil spread about the headstones by the wind, were John Brown the sexton and Mr Todge. They found a locket affixed by a metal chain to a shorn piece of dowelling from the shattered wreckage – they handed it in to Papa. You should have been there, Mr Aboyne."

"What an incredible addition to your sketch pad, your funerary archive. Are you peeved you missed such an episode? Please say you are, "Anne teased.

Charlotte, the eldest sister, remained more circum- spect. "Well, the whole lot's for the bonfire. She is to be cremated; the wood ash used as compost for rose bushes. Mind you, I think we could have fixed her up and put our bride on display and charge a penny per view. But why, I say, go to all that bother constructing such a kite?"

Gordon Aboyne offered certain other possibilities to be considered round the dining room table.

"Can we really say for certain, re-enacting a suicide was the intention? Was it more meant to be not taken quite so seriously? A joke, perhaps, or is there a deeper, hidden meaning we are all missing? What is the bride's true significance?"

"A joke in very poor taste, sir." Emily turned up her nose, twisting round, for while they were busy talking, unbeknown to them, the preposterous brother, Branwell, after stumbling down the staircase, had entered the parlour sinking in an available chair after an exhausting night. The wallpaper in his bedroom had been undulating demonic faces, morphing and twisting in a continuous state of flux.

"Fiends begone!" He had intoned miserably from his bed. "Leave me be that my torment be ended." But they did not, more and more emerged from the patterning, bearing hideous tusks at him. The ceiling swirling like a whirlpool, Dantes *Inferno* incarnate.

"You look in very poor shape," chided Charlotte, observing his shabby state, spectacles askew, matted, unwashed ginger hair, thin whiskers and the small growth of beard upon his chin tainted with remnants of food.

Tiger the snooty cat went by with his tail in the air.

Keeper growled, baring its fangs, hackles raised.

"What, pray, do you crave most in life upon this wondrous autumnal day, Branwell? Opium, a bottle of laudanum? Are you vying to become Haworth's answer to De Quincey? I've never seen you looking more yellow about the gills," said Charlotte pointedly.

"Stay thy sarcasm," he answered curtly. "Actually, a cup of tea would not go amiss, to ease my throat. Anne, dearest, would you oblige? You're nearest the pot."

He gave a congested cough and wheeled round to face the dried-peat fire, warming his trembling hands by the flames.

"How does your liver feel?" asked Anne, sarcastically.

"Pickled. After several pints of gin, thank you. Now pass me that cup, and less of your lip. How are you, Gordon? You prefer The Kings Arms to the Bull?"

"Frankly, I find the clientele at the Black Bull rather low brow, full of bovine farmers. I prefer not to drink with livestock."

"Boisterous, I'll give you that much. What about this locket you mentioned, Emily? What became of that novelty?" The brother gulped down scolding hot tea, dribbling on his chin.

"The locket is in Papa's study on his desk."

"Fetch it for me, will you Anne? Hup, hup, be quick."

"'Tis only an old cheap thing, hardly worth a farthing." Anne was fed up with the interruptions, she wanted to finish a watercolour of their other dog, *Grasper*, not be at beck and call to her useless bully of a brother. Branwell was a nuisance, always demanding attention. She heartily wished he'd hurry off to the snug at the Black Bull tavern and stay there for good.

"Fetch the locket damn you!" his voice thundered, pent up frustration the result of intoxicants *and yet another restless night wrestling wallpaper demons.*

Self-control abandoned, overwhelmed by rage, he flung the tea cup full pelt at the fire grate, with such force it shattered all over the fireplace. "Damn thee, do as I tell you, madam."

Even at this late stage in his addiction, abstaining from alcohol would prove beneficial to his health all round, but the effort required was so monumental it defeated his reason, he is preferring the easier route: drinking himself to death, and to hell with the consequences.

Abrupt mood swings, a persistent cough and lung catarrh. How much longer could his immune system bare this onslaught? A constant worry to his ever-caring father. The parson always held out hope that one day his son would change his ways and find redemption.

To save Anne from further annoyance, Charlotte (the eldest sibling) rushed off to the study. She was of diminutive stature, often shy in company, yet bore a fiery determination when riled.

"Gordon, old man, I have had a terrible night of it. Father tries so hard, but what's the use? I'm not long for this world. Might you do me the kindness of sketching me as I rest in an open coffin? An unlidded presentation should be truly splendid. Pen and ink, wax crayon, perhaps."

Aboyne, somewhat amused, nodded accordingly. He had heard this sort of tripe dozens of times. Branwell's morose pronouncements were legendary.

"I shall be posed in a final toast, a tumbler of grog held between rigored fingers, my corpse sat up, mouth wired in a pleasing smile by the undertaker, chalky skin, painted red lips, a clown's mask over my wooden features."

"I like that very much," quipped Mr Aboyne, helping himself to another biscuit. "Your inspired coffined tableau may yet win me entry into the Royal Academy Branwell."

The rest of the house guffawed at the sheer lunacy. Meanwhile, the silver-plated locket mercifully offered Branwell a useful distraction.

While the sisters were at last allowed to continue with their projects, Branwell sat fumbling with the locket for some twenty minutes. He managed to prise the locket open, discovering a lock of hair and a folded piece of tissue paper concealed within.

Freezing sleet and fog that normally engulfed Haworth in November, the blizzards of deep winter, had yet to prevail upon the Yorkshire mill town on the edge of the Pennines.

Although the rain that week proved heavy and persistent, so that damp seeped into the mossy stonework of the closely-knit cottages and shops either side of the steep cobbled street leading up to the church.

Five

In another part of town, peering out of the sash window of Mr Kenyon's detached villa, Dr Otley felt perfectly glad to remain indoors, so far spared the soaking he'd receive while doing his rounds on horseback later.

The presence of the physician enhanced Violet's feeling of contentment. Happiness was achievable, despite that cruel husband of hers living across the craggy moors above Haworth.

"We love one another, that is decided, "she proposed, in a delicate way, offering the doctor a slice of fruit loaf baked by cook in the range oven this morning. Sublimely easy in the company of her dearest acquaintance, she added: "What do you intend to do about it?"

"The law dictates that we cannot live together," he answered, brushing crumbs from the front of his waistcoat. "Although I wish that were not the case, the town registrar would deem otherwise." He paused, while plucking up the courage to say "Violet, *Cupid and the Butterfly* by Mr R.Yates is being staged in town on Saturday evening. Would you mind if I brought tickets for two... and would you care to join me?"

"I will." She paused "In saying the words 'I will' remind me that my marriage vows were a complete an utter sham. Mendelssohn's triumphal 'Wedding March', pah! Even before Sir James prised the gold band onto my finger, he was settled on an evil deed. I could not swim for the life of me, 'death by drowning' should have been incorporated into the marital vow."

The doctor, preferring to put his plate aside, leaned over, grasping his beloved's hand between his own. "Violet, dearest, as long as this matter remains unresolved, accusing Sir James of foul play, deliberately setting out to murder you, would be very difficult to prove after all this time has elapsed. It would most likely be thrown out of court. I believe you of course, but lawyers will likely regard the accusations as verging on hysterical. However, be that as it may, the die is cast. As you say, I must try to find a way to resolve the issue. If nothing else, for your own peace of mind."

"I see it all too clearly, Sam, every detail. I am aware of that detestable man kindly directing me toward the craft with a guiding hand at the nape of my back, me protesting, him attempting to seize me by the shoulders, determined to shove me overboard. I slip, my plimsolls skid on the wet deck. Was it the tiller I struck my forehead on? I'm not sure. It's just too frightful, I'm all dizzy, Sam." Her body slumped, dejected, reliving the entire experience.

"Don't vex yourself so, take a sip of tea and relax if you can."

"That man free to plunder my legacy, using it to his own advantage. Funding more factories to smog up the sky. While I would be more inclined to build an Italianate Garden or plan a deer park."

"Haworth has its fair share of mills, but look to Bradford, only eight miles distant, 12,000 hands in one hundred-and-eighty factories. The manufacture of textiles, muslins, cambrics, dimity, ginghams result in vast profits. Sir James has made himself a part of this revolution, a man of industry. But Violet, you mustn't allow this trying business to consume you, we have each other now. In some bizarre way, we have been brought together by your husband's behaviour."

"But for what? Shall we put a full stop to our love for each other, draw a line in accordance to the law? *I am a married woman*, therefore ..."

"No stop now. Now let me ... allow me please, to assemble the facts. Cannot your family lawyer, 'Old Hawley' assist you to obtain some kind of reasonable settlement? Alert him to the fact that you no longer wish to be wed? There must be a way out of this. A loophole of some sort, irreconcilable differences, a monetary settlement perhaps?"

"And true to form, true to his type, he should prove completely intransigent. Bitterly opposed to any settlement of any sort. Such a nest of wasps. The sting. The pain."

Six

That afternoon the rain eased. Having dealt with a number of patients and with no births pending, Dr Otley sought solace upon the moors to ponder the situation he faced.

In an oilskin cape and wide-brimmed hat, he rode his sweet-tempered dappled mare, Juniper, up the unmade rubble track, the horse clopping gently in the direction of Sleighton Beck.

Clusters of purple gorse dappled the scene. Gleaming wet blocks of granite emerged from the turf upon which horned sheep grazed; the occasional rocky waterfall shrouded in mist. Much appreciated features contributing to the majesty of the landscape.

Abruptly he drew on the reins, pausing to take in a small cottage.

Seizing his attention, a turnip headed scarecrow stood proud in the middle of a rough cabbage patch. The scruffy top hat and tails, a carnation made out of shredded paper pinned to a lapel – unmistakably, a bridegroom.

Otley dismounted, wandering up to the cottage to carry out a closer inspection of the straw-stuffed effigy.

A young fellow wearing a smock and gaiters, came out of the homestead, stood firm with arms folded he eyed his visitor warily.

"Good day, sir. Is this scarecrow your own handiwork?" asked Dr Otley.

"Aye indeed he is. Won't you come on in, share a pot of strong brew. I've put kettle on, it's no bother like. The sky's greyed right up, a proper downpour due."

"Thank you, I will," Dr Otley answered looking up. "Yes, it has darkened considerably. Dr Samuel Otley from the parish of Haworth." He removed his hat.

"John Hubbart, I farm a smallholding, like. Plenty of us up here on the moors scratching a living. Scraping by an' that," He ushered his guest across the threshold.

The doctor bowed his head passing under the old sagging doorway, politely standing aside to let John in behind him. "Well, Mr Hubbart, no sooner do I step through the door of your abode than I am witness to the clutter of a kite maker. Rolls of sailcloth, lengths of dowelling, boxes of tacks, a glue pot, a workbench by the window there." A simple nod was pointed his way in response, "I have heard and read much recently concerning the scarecrow bride. Are the two related, the one in your cabbage plot and the suicidal other half that the newspapers have made famous all over Yorkshire for jumping off the church tower?"

"Worse for them," said he, collecting clinking mugs, offering the doctor a chair over by the stone settle. "The truth of the matter was nowt to do wit' suicide, God forbid. Resurrection in the life 'ereafter more like. To float her onto clouds like. To see her play upon the breeze. Mary's pure soul. Alas, that mornin's gusts were so strong the strings holdin the kite bust. An' me, silly bugger, lost all control. Never meant fer her to plunge down t'earth. No, she were to soar upwards from that church. To release her into heaven like. From my vantage point, when I fust realised what had 'appened, I hurried t'church gates opposite Black Bull pub an' saw such commotion, a crowd 'ad gathered ont church path round by the plots where the poor folk get buried. Daft Halporth's inspectin' me kite ... all smashed up and ruined." He sniffed and wiped his nose with a dirty sleeve, "Oh but sir, the wurst of it, the very wurst of it, is that Mary's bridal gown and veil were in tatters, finished up on the very grave where they'd buried 'er but six weeks past. I scarpered, panicked I tell thee, straight to the Black Bull ta drown me sorrows."

This continual reference to 'Mary' jogged the doctor's memory. "Hubbart... I recall the name from a newspaper. Are you the same fellow who was to wed a mill girl, *Mary Belper*. Correct me if I am wrong and forgive any insensitivity, but she was killed in an industrial accident, just three days before your wedding. The horrific misfortune, a single thread of her long hair caught up and snagged in the roller of a belt-driven carding engine."

"She wer't dead, alright, ruined. They took 'er to the infirmary. Tis common knowledge that the factory owners failed ta install a wire guard. 'Ad they done so, Mary, might still be alive wouldn't she? Curse the lot o' 'em. Foreman, overlooker, office manager, mill owner – the blasted lot o' them."

"Tragic indeed. I am so sorry".

"Overlooker in't charge on't factory floor claims it were *her* fault fer not looking out. Nowt a word of apology nor condolence from the office. Business flourishes, thas what my Mary gave 'er life fer. To make men like Sir James bloody Grueldyke a packet o' brass. He owns Pegg Mill, what's 'ee care fer a gal like her?"

The conversation was interrupted abruptly as rain began to hammer down on the roof, water cascading down the windowpanes.

"Well, I find myself a fortunate fellow in passing by your home today," said the physician, doing his best to tactfully change the subject, "encountering your scarecrow bridegroom. The splendidly rigged partner of your well-crafted kite. Not, alas airborne or attracting a crowd though."

"That there scarecrow sir, stuck in't clay there, is me. Empty o' emotion. I find mesel these days but a husk full o' straw, turnip headed. I be a man right enough certainly, but I might as well be dead t'world since my Mary left. I'll be joinin' 'er soon mind, no doubt o' it. But there be work to do on God's earth afore they put me in with 'er. By 'eck there is."

Fig 2

Seven

Having completed household duties for the day, fastening winter capes and adjusting bonnets, the Brontë sisters (seen off at the parsonage door by Keeper the enormous, lolloping half-mastiff, a most intimidating guard dog who had singled Emily out for his unswerving devotion, but was notorious for getting upstairs and leaping on the girls' beds with gigantic muddy paws) sallied forth from their Georgian home Glebe House, to attend an afternoon tea invitation.

The path led down by leaning headstones, tinged green with moss, then past the church and on towards the wrought-iron entrance gates.

Beyond the gates, a quartet of taverns, the village stocks, Lambert's the drug dispensary and the Yorkshire penny bank at the top of the scarp, looking down Main Street.

Between the tumble of millworkers cottages and shops, could be viewed in the valley textile mills, with tall, smoky chimneys. More than ten mills operated alongside the River Worth. This is where most of the towns people found employment.

The sisters hurried down the hill to keep an appointment with Violet Kenyon (or Lady Grueldyke as she had been known before the accident) so recently restored to full vigour, whose housekeeper Mrs Leyden, had called the previous day with a card.

The autumn weather, typical for October, remained overcast

and dreary with a sharp, biting wind driving off the moor.

Admittedly Charlotte, Emily and Anne, whilst knocking at the front door to Mr Kenyon's fine detached house, were filled with a certain trepidation. After all they had, up till now paid charitable visits, used to glimpses of Violet confined to a bath chair like a waxwork, wooden and stiffly featured being wheeled about Haworth by Mrs Leyden. None were quite prepared to envisage her as an ordinary, radically changed person. So long had the poor creature been in a passive state of being.

"Why, you know Miss Kenyon wasn't a corpse," said Charlotte in hushed tones, waiting expectantly for the door to open.

"Though near enough," responded Emily, clutching her leather folder of drawings and watercolours (mostly of family pets) brought along as a pleasant diversion to be perused over.

The sisters were waiting for Mrs Leyden to answer the clanging of the wrought iron bell pull. It was not Mrs Leyden who answered, but Violet herself. And such a violet, full of mischief and life, greeting her friends on the pillar flanked porch with a flourish of hugs and kisses. Her heart aching to impart her romantic entanglement to the handsome bachelor Dr Otley.

Alas, as tea progressed, she misjudged the sisters' attitude and let forth about her experience in the Lake District. If this were not scandalous enough for prim, gentle ears, her present extra marital entanglement provoked the wrong response entirely.

Charlotte stared at her in disbelief, "You are a married woman! You cannot flout the law disobeying God's holy ordinance," said the elder sister haughtily.

"When, pray, are you to resume your proper role as the mistress of Scrivelsby Hall?" Asked Emily, "You are beholden to your husband,".

"Yes, to obey him, to worship him as a devoted wife," said Anne, showing the same intolerance.

Violet's features hardened, "Love, honour and obey *a fiend*? A fiend who attempted to kill me on our honeymoon? Who even, when facing each other by the altar uttering marriage vows, was plotting to see me drown in the lake? No. I think not, ladies. The idea of having my victuals poisoned while resuming my role at Scrivelsby Hall does not appeal to me one little bit. Nor shoved violently down the grand staircase. Neither being smothered by a soft pillow while abed to the accompaniment of Sir James whispering soft nothings in my ear." She fumed.

"We are, all of us, women bound by the convention of the society in which we ..."

"I must, and will, give clear vent to my feelings, Charlotte. I have no intention of being 'bound' by any conventions. Since my recovery, I feel a new woman, emboldened, strong and independent. I shall give my love to the man who gave so much to me when I remained silent and unresponsive. Somehow, when I awoke, I was allowed to be privy to his record of constant administrations, to be made instinctively aware of his one-pointed devotion to me alone. He, like my father, was determined I would recover and kept a constant vigil. Where, pray, was Sir James

Grueldyke during my purgatory? He was spending all of my grandfather's legacy buying and fitting out new mills with the latest steam-driven looms. No! I love Samuel Otley, and he does me in return. Nothing or no one shall stand in my way."

"Because you are an attractive woman, lest we forget," probed Emily, taking another slice of seed cake, while Mrs Leyden poured more tea, most amused by the conversation so far, more than aware of the tryst developing between her mistress and the doctor. That, she surmised, could not remain private for much longer.

"One of the greatest beauties in Yorkshire, acknow- ledged as such. Why there is not a photography shop between Bradford and Harrogate, that does not display a framed image of your likeness in its window," said Anne, shyly.

The elder sister, Charlotte, both shrewd and calculating when the occasion arose, provided her own insight into Violet's affair of the heart. "Dearest Violet, please take time to reflect. This murder attempt, might you have dreamt it all whilst in a depressed state of mind? I would hope that be the case. Your ill-sparking brain be wholly responsible for a type of phobia. The plot conjured up, as we do in a wakened state, for our novels. Yet we express these notions in our creative writing, our jottings in our books, our diaries, our drawings, all outlets for the powerful goings on inside our thoughts."

"My dears, I have expressed all I wish to express upon the subject of 'me and mine'. Let us allow a fresh topic to embellish our tea party. Anne, allow me look over those pictures in your folder."

Eight

Striking his stout ash stick repeatedly against the wet cobblestones, Mr Kenyon the architect was halfway up the steep slope of houses of Main Street when he caught sight of Sir James Grueldyke's estate manager, Thomas Adwalton. A plump and genial sort, lounging upon the window seat in one of the quaint tea rooms.

Mr Kenyon entered the shop and after brief formalities were exchanged, greeted his old acquaintance warmly. Ordering suitable elevenses, the two got talking agreeably.

Mr Adwalton, with his boyish optimism and ready wit, open ruddy face and friendly manner, soon became the ideal sponge to soak up Mr Kenyon's many outpourings. The old fellow began to helplessly unburden himself of certain concerns he had been bottling up since his daughter Violet's astonishing outburst at the supper table. He revealed his worries in a forthright manner, the estate manager honoured, he of all people, should evoke such confidences from a man he knew mostly at a distance, though he had come to know more amenably at the wedding.

"Sir James received my letter referring to his wife's miraculous recovery I trust?"

"He did, certainly, with his usual equanimity. A man steeped in business as he is, I would not call the master warm or emotional, but in his own gruff way, he expressed how pleased he was and that

Violet should be welcome back as the mistress of Scrivelsby Hall whenever she chose. Although Dr Otley's final word should be sought regards any endeavour to move her from her family home in Haworth where there was the advantage of specialist care by a respected medical practitioner. The somewhat odd reference you make, Mr Kenyon, of foul play on the honeymoon strikes me as absurd. Obviously, I should advise that your daughter must perhaps continue her recovery. Her memory may be unreliable. Perhaps she requires more time to heal." He paused while a waitress fussed over their table, then continued with mild indignance "A boating accident occurred on Derwent Water that summer, we all know that. Violet slipped and struck her head, we are aware of that too, but attempted murder is an outrageous accusation Mr Kenyon. Sir James, if my own memory serves me correctly, was the perfect gentleman throughout. He acted responsibly from the start, organising her evacuation from the Lake District and remained always by her side. Do you not agree, Mr Kenyon?"

"Yes. I am bound to," the architect sighed. "I think it likely that her sudden awakening into normal awareness has everything to do with this interpretation, a paranoid fixation against her husband. I am considering consulting a nerve specialist in London, though I doubt our family physician Dr Otley would approve. However we interpret her behaviour, a serious mental fissure appears to have developed in her mind, and even if to us it is fantastical nonsense, suffering an ill-sparking cranial organ, a normal relationship between man and wife for now, cannot be possible. The mistress of

Scrivelsby Hall had best remain in her father's care," said he, nervously.

"Wise. How sensible you are Mr Kenyon. A rational argument if ever, such that I would expect from a gentleman such as yourself. I shall, meanwhile, pass on your good wishes to Sir James who remains preoccupied with his mill ownership at present."

Nine

Mr Kenyon's elegant Georgian house, facing towards Keighley, was lit up by an array of globe oil lamps and candelabrum, the spacious drawing room presently providing the perfect romantic setting for a tryst. Outside, a hard frost had set in, the normally dreary rain and drizzle blown off the moors, held back by a cold front of air.

Meanwhile, enjoying an intimate embrace (her father out attending to business) Violet and Dr Otley were reclining upon a red ottoman, bathed by tranquil firelight. Leaning her head against his after exchanging tender words and kisses she gently teased, "Tell me more about your afternoon adventure on the moors, Samuel. Where were we? Your horse keeled over and expired during a thunderstorm, struck by lightning you were trapped beneath her flanks when a mad woman with wild hair and haggish features, wearing rags to hide her scrawny nakedness came at you bearing a cutlass."

"No. A trifle inaccurate. Juniper remains alive and kicking, I recall no such thunder, nor lightning, nor a cutlass-bearing hag," Dr Otley corrected with a smile.

"Very well, Samuel. You and your intrepid mare were clopping up the track and spied a lone cottage. I know the place, near Ugglebarnby Farm, 'The Lees' it's called. Though I have gone by there often, I never once caught sight of its occupant. Is that the sum of your afternoon's gallivanting?"

"Hardly, Violet. I was about to say," said he, changing his position so that he could lean over and grab his cigar case from the polished round table, "that this afternoon I became privy to the identity of the kite flyer responsible for the churchyard dramatics earlier this month."

"The scarecrow bride that was reported in all the papers. The whole of Yorkshire has been waiting with bated breath for the next instalment?"

"I have a continuation to the story. Now bear with me - I had a most enlightening encounter with a man named Mr John Hubbart, who farms the land thereabouts."

"Okay, elaborate."

"Well, I was startled to see a turnip-headed scarecrow dressed as a *bridegroom* in the middle of his plot of cabbages. Crossed sticks draped with an old top hat and tails, a white, paper carnation on the lapel."

"The partner, the mate of the straw-stuffed bride? The question we must ask ourselves, is why did she decide to fling herself off the church tower? Was her turnip-headed future husband being unfaithful, was she perhaps pregnant with a turnip by another agricultural suitor lurking in the corn field?"

"If only it were so frivolous. Mr Hubbart told me that the scarecrow suicide was not intentional that blowy morning. You see, what he meant to do was fly her aloft above the church and release her into the clouds – a celebration of the spirits ascendance into heaven. Alas, this did not go well. The scarecrow bride, incredible as it seems, was an effigy of his betrothed, Mary Belper, who was tragically killed three days before their wedding. An industrial accident to blame. She worked down at Pegg Mill in the valley. What a blow to deal with. The poor chap I found to be inconsolable, sick with grief, identifying more and more with the scarecrow he planted amongst the cabbages and less and less with his real self. I worry for his sanity, I really do."

"To me, the scarecrow bride and groom seem distinctly pagan," commented Violet, her views pleasing the doctor, for her intelligence clearly matched his own.

"The effigies do bring a pagan 'resonance', certainly. Living on the moors, the fellow is so isolated. As a doctor, I advised Mr Hubbart to seek company, had he perchance a sister who might come and keep house for a while. I left him some powders to help him sleep."

"I hope they can help in soothing his heavy heart. I met with Charlotte Brontë and her sisters today."

"You did?"

"She informs me the scarecrow bride will shortly be condemned to the bonfire."

There was a bang as the front door opened, the noise of bustling servants in the hall, Mrs Leyden attending to Violet's father arriving home.

He soon entered the drawing room, moving directly toward the coal fire to warm his hands, he had a troubled look about him.

"I have committed a terrible blunder," he said gruffly. "Otley, I am such a damned fool. I really did put my foot in it this time. I've disturbed a hornet's nest, so I have."

"Nothing a large whisky won't cure," said the physician, smiling warmly. "Douse the hornets."

"Very well, Doctor, if you prescribe it."

"I certainly do. Cigar?"

"I will have one of those also."

Violet burst out laughing. "Papa, you're so gentle and kind, even when you're riled. Why are you so serious? Has the world really crashed down upon the Kenyons?" she giggled. "I know what this is about. You visited Old Hawley, the solicitor, tonight and he proclaimed that I am worth precisely tuppence halfpenny, my fortune all squandered, frittered away, and you, dear father of mine are blaming yourself. Well don't. Sir James Grueldyke deserves the blame."

"This is no jest, my dear Violet. Heavens, were that the case, simply some financial indiscretion, I should happily leap in and out of the coal fire three times."

"Before I ring for tea, I must tell you Papa, Charlotte, Emily and Anne visited and requested, no, asked me to tell you that the Rev Patrick Brontë wonders if you might be able to draw up plans for an extension to the new schoolhouse."

"The vicar is my best and dearest friend. That is all very well and good, but Thomas Adwalton, he is bad, very bad indeed." Mr Kenyon puffed on his cigar thoughtfully.

"The estate manager," shrugged Violet, totally nonplussed, "I have always found him a bit of a buffoon. Mr Adwalton and his wife were very kind to me before the wedding. T'was he who first showed me about the house and grounds."

"Was he 'oh so very kind and affable'? Well, not anymore. If only he had not repeated what I told him in total confidence."

"Where?"

"At the tea shop."

"The tea rooms are surely rather public." Cut in Samuel.

"Be that as it may, Doctor, my letter to Sir James has been misinterpreted to his advantage. Damn my indiscretion, for now Old Hawley informs me a legal team is to be assembled. The machinery of the courts put into motion on a point of serious slander against Sir James Grueldyke."

Ten

The clock halfway up the stairs, kept in its own special niche and wound nightly, struck the half hour, proclaiming that all was well. The front door had been bolted by the vicar at nine, family prayers at eight.

The sisters huddled before the range with its copper urn and kettle, discussing the proposed route for a walk on the moors the following week, should the rain hold off. Tabitha the elderly servant was washing up at the sink. The evening winding down to a close.

The first indication of mischief occurred when Emily's mastiff quite abruptly leapt up on all fours. The giant hound barking furiously at those unseen as they approached Glebe House from Church Lane, then cutting across the garden lawn.

Uncouth laughter followed, thereafter by heavy thumps at the front door, the parsonage was under siege from a pair of merry drunkards.

If this was not infamy enough, somebody vomitted profusely on the porch steps, all seven of them. More retching, disgusting to the ears, more danger signals to alert those in the house that Branwell was home from the Black Bull, but he was not on this occasion alone.

The Rev Patrick Brontë, showing great courage, unbolted the door. Not surprised to discover the wild-haired, gin infused Gordon Aboyne miserably crouched over, supported by Mr Brontë's intoxicated son, mess spilled all down the front of his shabby suit.

"You'd better come in, the pair of you." The vicar indicated with an open hand towards the bannister at the foot of the staircase further down the hall, "Be so good as to pass onto the upstairs landing. You can spend the night in Branwell's room Gordon. A bowl of water, soap and towels shall be brought up presently to clean yourselves up. We'll supply you with a jug of hot cocoa to settle your digestion."

"Talking of digestion," Charlotte scolded, herself having entered the hall, observing first-hand the drunken wreckage about to stagger upstairs, barely able to cling onto the banister. "Mr Aboyne, be good enough to use the enamel potty under the bed if you should wish to further erupt the contents of your stomach. Neither we nor the servants, have any desire to clear up after you."

"Sirs," said Emily (equally scathing of the young men's behaviour) being of a more pompous tone than even her sister, "have the goodness and care not to break any furniture or ornaments on your way to bed."

Anne hurried back into the kitchen annoyed that their father should yet again be having to deal with his obnoxious excesses.

Branwell (once again) soon found himself drifting in a dreamy half-light hoping, no believing, that he was destined to strike a rich vein of fame through his writing.

Tonight, however, Branwell struck a rich vein of terror. Whilst his obliterated colleague snored onward, mug of milky cocoa long ignored, Branwell (the more regular imbiber of liquor) lay abed, unable to find oblivion. His vitals awash with poison, his mind forced awake, wrestling the writhing, hideous demons with tentacled faces that emerged like volcanoes from the wallpaper. In one instant male, the next female, all of them monstrous and scaly-skinned. More and more of the fluctuating beings taking up greater amounts of wallpaper space until, desperate to distract his sluggish awareness, for some practical task to occupy himself, he glanced around the room.

The gleam of the silver-plated locket and chain on his bedside cabinet, the one found by the shattered kite, propelled him away from the undulating wallpaper. He was reminded of the folded tissue paper, his keen intelligence attracted, above all, by the strange riddle written on its surface.

That same night, Dr Otley likewise found sleep illusive. He had only recently returned home after administering to a Mrs Baron (then living in a back-to-back cottage) for an inflammation in both legs, her limbs badly swollen due to dropsy.

A welcome distraction from an epic problem that had arisen due to Mr Kenyon's loose tongue at the tea shop, where he had naively repeated his daughter's accusation that Sir James had been guilty of attempted murder on their honeymoon. This, to of all people, the estate manager, a person in daily converse with his master.

The matter was serious, for now Sir James Grueldyke of Scrivelsby Hall was preparing to mount a legal challenge to question his wife Violet's state of mind. Resolutely determined on having her committed to an asylum to be kept under observation.

Mr Kenyon's indiscretion had cost them dearly. There again, how long before the torrid affair between himself and so-called Lady Grueldyke, the mill owner's wife, became public knowledge. One of the father's servants was sure to blab sooner or later. A couple attracted to one another cannot conceal their affection for long from the gossips!

The clock upon the mantelpiece chimed one. Despite the lateness of the hour Dr Otley decided to abandon the fireside to take an invigorating nightime stroll to clear his head, and to mull over the almost insurmountable problems that were quickly engulfing his world.

He must strengthen his resolve. Much too agitated for slumber and knowing his servants were all in bed, he went out to the hall stand and donned his riding coat, scarf, gloves and wide- brimmed hat.

Seizing his silver-topped cane from the cracked China vase used as an umbrella stand, he departed the front door, instantly aware of the increasing low temperature. A hard frost had settled over Haworth, his exposed face chilled within moments of quitting the house. Clanging shut the front gate Dr Otley strode quickly, glad to be in motion, the soles of his boots crunching underfoot creating imprints on the speckled white pavement.

"We shall succeed ... we must succeed, "he muttered between gritted teeth, refusing to be cowered. Might not 'Old Hawley' the family solicitor, have a trick up his sleeve?

Best foot forward, a brisk uphill trudge to the top of Main Street, round by the bank, then along by Haworth church was the preferred route. Apart from the occasional, bracketed lamp casting a meagre glow over the cobblestones, dwellings remained dark.

Having finally crested the hill, the last person on God's earth the physician expected to encounter as he strode past the church gates was Branwell Brontë.

Observing the bespectacled figure wearing only a nightshirt, loitering on the church path, leaning up against the inert railing between one of the four squat pillars, the doctor rushed up the steps.

"Branwell," he hissed, plumes of his smoky breath visible in the freezing air. "It is I, Dr Otley. What are you doing out here? You're not even wearing a coat or a scarf. Do you want to catch the death?"

"The grim reaper and I be already on cordial terms."

"Do you not realise a hard frost has set in, Branwell?"

"I damn well need a sounding board. I must have a sounding board. Gordon's sound asleep, so he's a fat lot of good. I tried to shake him awake earlier, but no luck. Otley… I think I'm onto something, if only I could grasp the crux."

"Have you been taking laudanum, eating hashish? Are you aware of the air temperature? In your present state of dress, you could catch pneumonia. Does your father know you are wandering about out here?"

"I'm not intoxicated, I am more rather *innovated*. Father would be pleased, encouraged, I think."

"Very clever, Branwell. Listen young man, I volunteer to be your blasted sounding board, if you promise me you will come back to my house this instant. How long ago did you last drink gin, or whatever?"

"Dunno. Tennish? In the snug of the Black Bull."

"Very well. Here, I'll help you through the gates.

For heaven's sake, we must get you in front of a good fire. We can take the short cut down the alley to reach my house."

With a firm step, the physician seized Branwell's arm. Like a boisterous child, the nightgown-clad reprobate seemed impervious to cold, marching down the hill with a swagger, although once indoors, the warmer environment caused him to develop a hacking, chesty cough. Worryingly, the doctor alerted to a shortness of breath, wheezing, congestion, Branwell was undoubtedly in failing health.

Disappearing into another room, Otley re-entered with a thick blanket which he draped over his patient's arched shoulders before attending to the fire. "Allow me to carry out an examination, to strike your chest, prepare you a compound at least," he suggested, heaping on coals from the scuttle. The visitor, slumped in his chair, was indignant.

"Damn your quack remedies. There's far more important matters to concern ourselves with. I require an interested listener, nothing more. Hear me out Dr Otley."

"Look here, I'm going to sit on this armchair, smoke a pipe and give you my full, undivided attention. Why, you may even encourage me to have forty winks, which I could really do with right now."

Smiling, Branwell burst into a fit of coughing, but when sufficiently recovered, removed from his pocket a silver-plated locket attached to a metal chain. The wavering firelight gleamed on its reflective surface.

"This little find should rightly be in my father's study. However, by way of curiosity, I purloined it myself. Thereafter in the presence of my illustrious sisters, I prised open the compartments. No pictorial images are evident of a sweetheart, but! We do have a lock of her hair. That… and a folded square of tissue paper."

"Yes, I'm with you."

"This locket was discovered entangled with bits of snapped wood supporting the bridal gown, the broken flying contraption so christened 'the scarecrow bride'. You no doubt saw the headlines in the *Halifax Guardian*."

"Indeed."

"John Brown, my father's long-time sexton and dear family friend, handed the locket in. The object is of no real value, yet the square of tissue paper is worthy of closer scrutiny. Tonight while lying in bed, I was seized by a truly astonishing possibility. Tell me what you make of it."

"Naturally, I had no idea this locket existed." The doctor's features appeared to waver and flicker in the light of the flames from the fire.

Unfolding the square of paper, the doctor was delighted to find a few words written in black ink, partly blotted into the whole. Removing his clay pipe from his mouth, he read it aloud:

The day after the Sabbath
The last in October
At twelve
Thy will be done
I am
The Resurrection

"You are acquainted with the writings of Thomas De Quincey."

"I read his *Confessions of an English Opium Eater* in *The London Magazine*. He is a clever stylist. Although I fear his sensational prose encourages a cult like following. You yourself are one are you not Branwell?"

"Mayhaps I am. I am referring not so much to De Quincey's opium writings. But another piece on murder, considered as one of the fine arts."

"I beg to differ; most murders seem to me brutal and vapid. Explain where this be leading old fellow, you obviously have some sort of bee in your bonnet. Why else would you wander out into an exposed churchyard on a winter's night wearing only a nightshirt?"

Branwell, paused. Collecting himself before continuing, "Viewed practically, the scarecrow bride is basically a clever kite. The only man known round here for building kites in an array of sizes is a Calvinist by the name of John Hubbart. I don't have a clue about him, bar what I read in a newspaper account when I was a railway clerk. The *Leeds Mercury* mentioned a John Hubbart in relation to a mill worker he was due to marry. She was killed in an industrial accident."

"I know the circumstances well. He is a tenant farmer over at

Ugglebarnby."

"I've since learnt that the moor folk have become disturbed recently by a queer scarecrow effigy kitted out as a bridegroom that made an appearance outside his cottage last week. So I put two and two together."

"Congratulations, Branwell. The bride *and the groom*. What else?"

"John Brown, my father's sexton and family friend who I drink with at the Black Bull told me he was informed that after the accident, Hubbart lost his reason and began behaving oddly. He holds Sir James Grueldyke, the owner of Pegg Mill, wholly responsible for the needless death of his betrothed, Mary Belper. What do you think that tells us Doctor?"

Otley placed his hand to his chin in thought, before continuing, "That Hubbart bares a grudge, a deep grudge, that he could fly off the handle, and potentialy murder Sir James. Dear God Branwell this is serious. I remember, no hint of an apology, nor offer of compensation from the work's office. Enough to tip a man over into thoughts of retribution? Bureaucracy at its very worst in the face of human tragedy. Not for the first time nor the last either in this industrial empire."

Branwell agreed with a morose nod, gazing solemnly into the flames of the fire, crossing his legs, folding his hands together. For once, acting like the intelligent man he really could be and not an obnoxious slob.

"Consider, Dr Otley, if you dare. John Hubbart *will be*, is bound to, seek revenge for his girl's death. The writing in the locket, cloaked in biblical phrasing, represents a statement of intent. The last Sabbath in October is now past, this then be the day of reckoning. The note tells us everything. What it doesn't tell us is whether twelve o'clock refers to noon or midnight?"

Prior to the mantelpiece clock striking three, sat in their armchairs, lamp glasses smoke-filled dark and dingy, candles low, much exhausted by continuous debate as to whether the crime was to be instigated at twelve midday or twelve midnight, the pair finally judged midnight the more likely time to murder Sir James. For the simple reason it would be dark. The servants in bed, Scrivelsby Hall would be silent and approachable, the grounds easier to access. Branwell had heard, courtesy of a quarryman at the Black Bull, that John Hubbart was a skilled poacher who knew well the lay of the land thereabouts.

Dr Otley, however much as he personally loathed the mill owner, felt it his avowed duty as a medical practitioner (under the Hippocratic oath) to support life, not by sleight of hand encourage a murder he might prevent.

If this obscure writing upon the folded paper did indeed refer to an assassination he must, and would, do everything in his power to thwart any attempt.

An urgent intervention was required. He must ride over to Ugglebarnby Farm and bring sensible argument to bear. Anything to prevent John Hubbart from committing murder and going to the gallows.

Alternatively, Otley might discover the cryptic message unrelated, but what cared he for embarrass- ment? Better that than, allowing for the matter to go unchecked, unchallenged.

The doctor knocked out his pipe, preparing to go to bed. Branwell had finally found oblivion and sleep after his gallant excursion on behalf of the silver-plated locket.

The physician banked up the fire, heaping on more coal and acquired more blankets to wrap around the frail, bespectacled figure.

He noted the stertorous breathing, Branwell's pallor a tell-tale yellow relating to the liver, the hacking cough he had born all night. might he be tubercular? If so, the end would not be far off.

Eleven

A late breakfast finished, while his horse was being saddled Dr Otley felt if a reasonable argument should prevail, Hubbart might yet be prevented from taking a doomed course. Otley himself was in a quandary. He owed Sir James Grueldyke no favours, he was in no way particularly enamoured towards the mill owner and frankly, felt he lacked conviction carrying out his enterprise. But he was bound by his moral duty to act, given that twelve midnight was the preferred hour for assassination. Both he and Branwell had decided this left him plenty of time to intervene.

However, if Branwell's core deduction concerning the riddle inside the locket proved unsound, wildly off the mark, the writing pertaining to a totally unrelated matter, then he was about to get egg on his face, his journey would prove a wasted (and embarrassing) muddle!

Mounting his horse, he patted his mare *Juniper* fondly, as together, man and beast sought to attain the higher ground leaving Haworth, following the ancient road and packhorse tracks beyond Ponden Kirk across the moors.

The wild terrain was dotted with grazing sheep. The ground littered with rocky boulders, clusters of heather and purple flowering gorse. It was upon one of these roads a meeting of great minds took place, for he was profoundly glad to see Violet Kenyon riding towards him.

He raised his hat, and they craned over to kiss one another – as much in love as ever.

"What an errand I am on," said he, leaning off his horse, planting another kiss on her cheek.

"Well, I have been riding all morning and am much invigorated. My dear Samuel, to where be you headed? Visiting a patient, I'll warrant."

"In a manner of speaking, a serious twist concerning that blaggard Sir James Grueldyke."

"My father has taken steps to engage Old Hawley, our trusted lawyer. He is periwigged and wears Georgian clothes and must be eighty-six if a day... but his mind is as sharp as a razor. He has an eye to launch a legal broadside. Our solicitor has received no papers concerning slander or committal as yet, but insists my own startling, sensational experience on my honeymoon translated into newsprint would damn Sir James in the public mind, his reputation may be stained black and villainous in Yorkshire for perpetuity, his name would appear headlined in countless newspapers thus being enough to ward him off from approaching a Justice of the Peace."

"A view held by me also, although I fear I must concern you with a separate development. As much your business as mine. More so, in fact."

"Pray what is it Dr Otley?"

"That there exists a strong possibility someone may be out to murder your husband. Quite likely at the stroke of midnight."

"You have proof?"

"Branwell Brontë …"

"Branwell!" Violet exclaimed. "Oh, I knew him when he was younger and more level-headed. He was a fine gent then, taking after his clerical father. He was industrious, training with the artist William Robinson, hoping to enjoy a career as a portrait painter. He often begged me to sit for life studies. I declined, of course. Now, his brain is addled by drink, and I despair for him. Is he reliable? Can he really be trusted? He was sacked from the railway only last month."

"Branwell is sick Violet, I fear tubercular, yet he maintains a strong intellect, is highly creative and has had some poems published recently. He is not all bad. I believe a lady of mystery is at the heart of his torment. That said, his continual usage of laudanum may have opened his mind, allowing him a unique perception. He is an advocate of De Quincey."

"Very well, what has Branwell perceived then that has a bearing on this matter?"

"A lady's locket was found amongst the broken wood of the bell tower kite. I had no inkling. Branwell told me he discovered a lock of hair and a riddle inside – a cry for help, an act of desperation. The last thing I want is for this poor fellow to end up being turned off at the gallows."

"I am in absolute agreement, Sam. Sir James Grueldyke is hardly worth the price. Who is this person?"

"Accompany me to Ugglebarnby Farm and I will show you. There, my sweet turtle dove you will have your answer."

Violet gave him a bashful look. What a jaunty figure she presented. In a voluminous feathered hat, a superbly cut three-quarter length black riding coat, long skirt, and boots. A member of the local hunt, an accomplished equestrian and her abilities seemed not to have deserted her, despite the brain injury.

The weather for the ride was cloudy and blustery, driving occasional drizzle falling. Upon sighting the habitation, Dr Otley observed the chimney pot issued no smoke. More pertinently, the pagan-like effigy of the scarecrow was gone, nowhere to be seen.

With mounting dread, trying to stay calm, he took out his gold repeater, a gift from his late father, from the deep pocket of his riding coat. Flipping open the lid, he studied the watch face intently. It was a quarter to twelve, midday.

The realisation hit him like a bolt of lightning - the twelve referred to in the note was in fact noon, not midnight.

"John Hubbart, are you there?" he shouted. "It's Dr Otley."

Silence was the firm reply.

"Hello... we be your allies, your friends," added Violet, peering about, no sign of movement.

The physician knew the futility. The homestead was deserted.

There would be no answer from John Hubbart now, maybe ever. They turned their horses hastening away, leaving that lonely place at a steady gallop.

That region of moorland is home to quarrymen, weavers and farmers. Down in the deep hollow of the beck lies the north country seat of the Grueldykes.

A pinnacled, gabled stone manor house of two storeys with mullioned windows, a Norman-style arch above the porch. Weather-worn tiles with the roof bearing clusters of chimney stacks. The three-hundred-year-old dwelling was offset by a rectangle of lawn bordered by close clipped hedges and trees bent back by the strong winds of the Yorkshire Pennines.

Passing lichen-stained gateposts capped with stone urns Violet and Dr Otley, from their vantage point sat astride their horses, had a fine view of the old house.

Violet found this unsettling, for she had not been here for nearly a year.

A man came running up and grabbed the reins of Violet's horse. A chubby, beetroot-complexioned fellow named Jack Tuxford, one of the gamekeepers.

"Why do you look so anxious, Jack?" She said in a kindly way.

"Mistress..." he replied with pleading eyes, his manner most curious, "An accident or summat. You'd best hurry quickly to thy hoose. I Messel' 'um waitin' further word."

Once the pair galloped up the drive, they were witness to a murmuring assemblage of house staff and estate workers gathered out front. A couple of sheeted stretchers brought lumberingly across the field from the treeline were deposited on the rough turf. Every flat cap and bowler removed in respect of the taller, lankier body.

Another burly figure hurried over, accosting the pair of horse riders in a firm but courteous way.

"Gosh, be ye Dr Saltburn from Keighley? If so, you must have ridden like the devil, summat of a record. I only sent old Callum fair ten minutes past in the trap."

"No sir, I am Dr Otley from Haworth. Can I be of assistance in any way?"

"Mistress," he nodded towards Violet, "please coom at once, and you also Doctor."

A number of men steadied the horses allowing them to jump down.

Once walking alongside the doctor, the man gabbled, "The master being nobly raised, like a dying Nelson at Trafalgar below decks, was supported by Mr Flodden, Mr Thirsk, myself and Thornby, the young beater. 'Wakefield, old lad,' he says, 'I'm done for. Make ready that stout oak coffin.' Those were his last words before he expired. I was by his side, brave to the last he was. A true gentleman."

"What, in bed? Had he been ill long," the doctor probed, trying to conceal his excitement.

"No, no, no, ee were out shootin' pheasant, sir. A madman run amok among us as the party wer't about to take lunch. A haybox set upon trestles, ee dug a great knife in 'is guts. A guest, Lord Mackleton, shot the villain dead wit both barrels. We were all of us taken by complete surprise. Ee were tha' quick, I'll give him that."

Both Violet (or Lady Grueldyke) and her companion Dr Otley showed a respectful nod to the body of Sir James.

At Violet's request, the assailant's corpse was unsheeted, Dr Saltburn from Keighley, the squire's personal physician, the official medical examiner had still to arrive.

"Whatta my to make o' this, sir? Fair flummoxed the lot o' us." The tarpaulin was soaked through with blood. "Steel yersel', the sight will be shocking madam. Aye, that it will, God 'elp us."

"I am a medical practitioner, Mr Wakefield," Otley reminded him with due gravitas. "Well used to gunshot wounds and the like. Do have done and be quick about it. Her Ladyship will require to see the estate manager – urgently."

"I meant thee no disrespect, Doctor, but what's ta make o' this?"

As the sheet was drawn back, it must be said Dr Otley sympathised and understood the crowd's revulsion, how they instantly drew away, for where the facial features normally would dominate, was a crude, pulpy mask carved out of a split apart mangel-wurzel root vegetable. It had been gutted out and given gashes for eyes and mouth. This whole facial disguise was tied to the back of the deceased's head with brown twine. A battered top hat worn above a knot of yellowed leaves sprouting from fibrous stalks of the hollowed-out vegetable acting as hair.

Certain garment's rescued from a rubbish heap (Dr Otley knew already about from his visit to the cottage) the frayed black tails, the blood-stained paper carnation destroyed – a pair of baggy, over-short opera trousers, huge, mouldy hob-nailed boots coming apart at the seams.

Thus, the scarecrow bridegroom made flesh John Hubbart's

spirit, free to join his sweetheart Mary Belper, floating forever in the cloudy sky above Haworth church.

Hallmarks and indicators of a pagan ritualistic right of spiritual crossing.

Twelve

Autumn passed. On the morning of Christmas, the three bells at Haworth church tower rung in unison, the Rev Patrick Brontë led his brood of daughters down the parsonage steps, across the lawn and through the gate in the wall.

Together they descended along the path, wading in the thick snow that had blown in for much of the night, settling everywhere and smothering the slab-top graves under a frozen crust of white, capping the groups of upright headstones and carved masonry monuments quite prettily. A real yuletide picture postcard painting.

Although the worst of the snow ceased around seven, the chill wind kept up its strength, blowing off the bleak moorland stretching to the west. Unsheltered by trees and situated at the top of the scarp the church, like Glebe House further up, was exposed to the elements.

On their way to church, the Brontë's chatted, for the most part about a pleasant evening spent at the Black Bull, where the night before a large commodious room was made available for the Haworth Philharmonic Society to put on a concert of Haydn, Emily and Anne being themselves both accomplished pianists.

"Those two be in love," said the vicar, poking young Anne in the ribs. "Emily come on now, don't look so stern. I talk of the young doctor who accompanies my friend Kenyon's daughter everywhere. Seldom out of each other's sight according to Mrs Leyden. Is that at all proper?"

"Violet and Dr Otley were holding hands at the Haydn performance," replied Charlotte, fixing her bonnet against the blustery wind, not caring a fig.

"Were they, indeed," answered the vicar good humouredly. "And so soon after the unfortunate ..."

"Murder," said Anne, a wisp of a woman, so slender one wondered if she might be blown away on a gust of wind. "Murder at Scrivelsby Hall... or at least on the shoot," added Emily, confidently.

"Well, less said about *that* the better," sighed Charlotte. "It is Christmas, after all."

But Christmas or not, the undercurrent of talk in the Yorkshire mill town (especially to simple, trusting folk) was still surrounding the slaying of Sir James Grueldyke, the last of the Grueldykes, by a scarecrow.

"Heavens above," exclaimed the vicar absent- mindedly, "did I, or did I not, order in a bumper of port and sherry wine. I am hosting after-church drinks, am I not? Does Tabitha, our servant, know of this?"

"I did it for you, Papa," replied Emily pertly. "Purchased from Thomas Bros last week. I put in the order on your behalf."

"Splendid, splendid. Not only be you a first-rate pistol shot (Emily and her father regularly practised with a target card in the nearby field, using his trusty flintlock) but an accomplished organiser to boot. What would I do without you, my dear?"

Peering from behind wire-rimmed spectacles with tiny oval lenses, the Rev Patrick Brontë found his eyes watering profusely, dazzled by the brightness of the snowy landscape, looking to the summit of Main Street.

"Now, where have those pair of turtle doves got to," said he, searching around. "Violet and the doctor, I refer to. Mayhaps gone into church I expect. Let us catch up with old Mr Kenyon. See, he dawdles by the porch."

The interior of Saint Michael's was always a trifle gloomy, lit by six large windows either side, the west window failing in winter to allow much natural light. A hugely antiquated structure, a dark, old oak three decker pulpit with a tasselled lectern overlooking rows of pews, looked positively funereal.

Festive Yuletide evergreens added cheer, the coke braziers placed at intervals along the aisle added on that freezing cold Christmas morning, a minimal amount of heat. Yet two people sat towards the back of the church, cared not a jot about how cold it was.

After competing with others of the congregation in a rousing rendition of 'Ding Dong, Merrily on High', accompanied by the wheezing harmonium, upon retaking their seats, Violet and Dr Otley whispered to one another, kneeling upon hassocks. "How unutterably strange and diverse be the path of true love. I am constantly amazed," said she, squeezing his hand.

"Violet, I am also. You are now the mistress of Scrivelsby Hall."

"Yes, but Samuel, if you are not there with me …"

"I will be, dearest. You know I will be."

Thirteen

A Fortnight Later...

The parsonage dining room that morning was alive with good humour, a haven for idle chatter. Tabitha Aykroyd, the Brontës live-in maid, bustled hither and thither from the kitchen with fresh pots of tea. There was a good blaze in the grate, the recesses on either side of the mantelpiece filled with books, the carpet and rugs composed of Kidderminster weave.

Branwell, red tousled hair a mess, for once clear headed and sober, came down from his studio at around eleven. Using a portable easel he was determined to finish a painting of his begun in '34, a portrait showing his three sisters.

Gordon Aboyne, one of three sat round the pedestal table, was in talkative mode, eager to reveal his latest portfolio of sketches entitled 'The Cemetery Wanderer' to Emily (and most especially Charlotte).

Further along the hall could be heard Anne exercising her fingers on the piano whilst her father sat at his desk busy with church matters, Haworth was a demanding parish. She played a clunky rendition of Mozart's variations in G, on a Dutch song by Graaf.

Tipping his hardback chair, leaning back precariously, and tugging his friend's sleeve Mr Aboyne was moved to say half in jest, "Branwell, old fellow, you wield a brush most skilfully. The National

Portrait Gallery is the place to hang that. I'll put in a good word if you like," he grinned.

Branwell, never satisfied, scowled intently before replying. "I've a real mind to 'do a Turner' on it and smudge the whole thing more into a blur. It strikes me as boringly competent. I yearn to express an abstracted vision."

"Stay your destructive hand," pleaded Gordon. "The portrait I like very much. You've caught the girls as good as anything."

"I look a right old mopey frump," complained Charlotte in mock despair, unfolding her pair of lorgnette eye glasses before passing a sheaf of Gothically inspired drawings to Emily.

"Now, Charlotte," said Mr Aboyne, nestling closer, "tell me what you make of this woefully grotesque family tomb. A superb mortuary monument I chanced upon at a church just outside Halifax."

Miss Brontë put on her glasses. "But what of this?"

"What of what?" he responded, mildly confused, peering where her finger lay.

"The figure, the queer image near the ilex tree that you've enhanced, shaded in with charcoal. What is it? A ghost, a goblin?"

Branwell ceased his painting to listen. Gordon remained at a loss.

"The deuce! Did I draw that? No, I didn't, couldn't have." He scratched his brow. "Nobody, I ever recall, was stood over by the ilex."

"Yet you must have put the image to paper. The detailed drawing of the overly decorated tomb is all there."

"For the life of me, I cannot fathom ... Why, on closer inspection, I am reminded of ..."

"The scarecrow bride."

"Oh, that's her," remarked Emily, much intrigued. "The turnip head. Look, the veil and the gown."

"That's definitely her," agreed her elder sister vehemently.

Quick to offer his viewpoint, Branwell proposed a psychosis of some kind. "Our subconscious. How fascinating," the brother admitted. "Thus, my dears, young Mr Aboyne, *totally unaware*, soaked in his preoccupation with death and cemeteries has created, unwittingly, a 'spirit drawing'. The bride appears on the page after manipulating our impoverished, drug-addled artist from *the beyond*, using him as a puppet, willing him to form her likeness upon the page."

"What rot!" laughed Emily, fully scathing of such high blown pontificating, calling Keeper who was impatient for his morning walk.

Once out the door she and her dog were romping along the lane up onto the moor. The hound (only recently forgiven for bounding upstairs, leaving muddy paw marks over freshly-made beds which resulted in a sound thrashing, for Emily could be formidably aggressive when she chose) became giddy with anticipation, due to good training he remained at heel, despite the prospect of rabbits, squirrels or even a cat to pursue.

Back in the house Tabitha, the elderly servant, a great favourite of the family, poured Charlotte more tea from the pot, before moving on to the study to replenish the vicar's cup – she paused to argue what constituted a real ghost.

"Tha' silly bride were a kite, a toy, nowt anything like a spirit," she was adamant. "Nowt like a headless horseman what rides all over t'moors on a fiery-eyed steed an' lopped off old quarryman's head!"

"Barefaced tosh." Branwell mixed more paint onto a pallet. "A silly Yorkshire fable."

"Nay, 'tis truth," replied the servant, feeling put out, once more open to ridicule.

"You see Tabby, an act of the subconscious, Mr Aboyne's, somehow without realising, putting pencil to paper and sketching an image of the bridal scarecrow, is significant – a real example of an artist possessed."

"Do give over, old man. You're making me nervous," quaked Gordon, eager to change the subject, yet a lapse of memory of events on his part was worrying. How, indeed, did the scarecrow bride end up being featured in his sketchbook? Wasn't that the day of the countryside funeral?

There came a persistent knock at the front door to Glebe House, and shown in were Mr Kenyon, a regular visitor, and his younger sister – Violet's Aunt Edie, or, more properly, Mrs Welland. While Mr Kenyon, the architect, hurried to the study for a chat with his dearest friend, the Rev Brontë, about some school building extension, his sister, Mrs Welland, was put in amongst the young folk.

Normally of a most lively, happy disposition, eager to join in with pranks, the sisters, particularly Charlotte, sensed something was amiss – the woman was out of sorts, she appeared pale and taciturn. *How unlike her.*

The loud debate concerning the scarecrow bride taking possession of Gordon Aboyne's talent as a sketcher prompted her to stiffly take her seat and, while removing her bonnet, herself pass comment.

"Oh, that poor mill girl, tugged right through a carding machine by a thread of her own hair, and thence the mad follow-up. Sir James Grueldyke struck dead within his own grounds. The papers were full of it, wanted the scarecrow saga to run and run."

"By the Calvinist."

"Yes, that lone, deranged man of the moors. Yet I sympathise, I really do. Oh Charlotte," she sobbed, "what about Mr Trowbridge?" She dabbed a hanky to her eyes.

"Cup o tea, Mrs Welland," offered Tabby, rattling the tray. "Things nevva look s'bad after a good old brew, d'they, lass?"

Mrs Welland clasped her hands together and attempted to smile.

"My dear lady," asked Branwell, lightly dabbing a layer of paint onto canvas with his brush, "I do not wish to pry, but it does one good to talk about these things rather than bottle them up. Who is this Mr Trowbridge, why be you so affected? Where has your usual cheery self-disappeared to this noon day."

"Our *dearest* Mrs Welland," said the elder sister.

"Notable for stitching those fine, decorative hassocks for the church pews," smiled Emily. "That folk are so pleased to kneel upon on Sundays."

"I suffered an awful shock, that's what," Mrs Welland answered bluntly. "Do you young people really want to know what us senior citizens get up to?"

"Do tell."

Charlotte and Emily nodded encouragement across the table. Gordon was patently relieved, for at last the matter of his being possessed got dropped.

"To begin with, I had met in the last month a very kind and affectionate elder gentleman by the name of Mr Trowbridge. We were compatible. I am, as you know, a specialist lace cleaner and mender. Gold and silver muslins, coloured embroidery of great rarity and quality. I can restore and revitalise cloths. You know all this, and that I am a most respectable widow of a solicitor I might add. No tongues are caused to wag upon my account. Mr Trowbridge and I were attracted to one another – fell in love if you will. Mark you, entirely open. We met at a splendid tea shop in Oxenhope village each Wednesday and Friday. That is until ..."

"Yes?"

"My suitor failed to turn up. So unlike him. Naturally, I became anxious, my temper out of sorts, for being 'stood-up' is intolerable. Furious, I stormed out of the shop and enquired whereabouts in the village could be found a certain Mr Trowbridge. A lady at the post office was kind enough to put me right. Thus, ten minutes later, following a brisk walk, I found myself at a most distinguished cottage. Promptly attaining the porch, I was fully expecting Mr Trowbridge to appear, cowering with excuses. Instead, maybe mistaking me for some other, I was ushered into a front room by a pair of overly concerned women. The place was both neat and furnished. However, the gloom, the ominously drawn curtains made the hairs on the nape of my neck prickle. I noticed a mirror draped in black bombazine, was alerted to the scent of lilies. Four tall flickering waxen candles feebly lit a scene of absolute horror. For there, central to the fireplace, resting upon trestles, I beheld an open wood coffin – taffeta-lined and adorned with brass fitments. Lying inside was my own Mr Trowbridge himself, very stiff and very, very dead. I babbled my sympathies, before rushing from the place. What can one do, having found *true love and bereavement* in the same week? Now you comprehend why I sympathise with that Calvinist character."

"At first the public believed the scarecrow bride represented …"

"*Suicide*, and dammit, I felt suicidal, and still do. I identify with the moorland farmer's torment. I do not condone his atrocious murder of Sir James, of course."

"You received no hint of illness? Mr Trowbridge having a weakened condition?" enquired Charlotte tactfully.

"None. From what I can gather, he rode regularly, both horses and a velocipede. One must take into account, I am not strictly a relative, a member of the family, but a recent acquaintance. Thus, I felt it improper to intrude further. I should never, ever have shown up at the funeral. Of course, I wouldn't."

"Gracious," exclaimed Gordon Aboyne, rummaging frantically through his sketchbook. "I was over at Oxenhope church last week. Might that be the very funeral you talk of?" He gazed, suddenly transfixed by the image of the scarecrow bride over by the ilex tree. A group of mourners gathered round a grave with the presiding vicar which he had drawn.

"'Nother cuppa Mrs Welland? Thy's bin proper hard done by alright."

"I will. Thank you, Tabitha," she answered, admiring the canny servant's broad Yorkshire accent. "I suppose I shall just have to try and get over it."

Fourteen

Adjacent to the old stocks, in fact, not very far from the flight of steps leading up to the church gates, is situated the Black Bull tavern. One of four hostelries doing business on that area of high ground. The Cross Inn, the Old White Lion and the Kings Arms (used as a courthouse when in session) being the remainder. The Black Bull, so close to home, was a cornerstone of Branwell Brontë's life.

For most of the day, in the presence of Mrs Welland, he sought to be courteous, attentive, a pleasure to be with and sensitive to her loss. Unfettered by opiates, hashish and brandy fireballs, his true nature allowed briefly to exist.

Alas, this interlude of commendable sobriety was but short-lived. By seven o' clock, ensconced in the snug at the Black Bull, surrounded by his boisterous cronies buying round after round, old habits swiftly returned. He and Gordon Aboyne were the worse for wear guzzling copious amounts of liquor, as indeed did the sexton of the parish - a friend of the family to be counted on - John Brown, who lived close to the parsonage, married with a daughter.

By nine o' clock, windows of the public house aglow, the clatter of tankards, the clink of glasses became noisier and noisier. A rising crescendo of jolly singing abounded that might be heard by anybody walking by.

By half past ten under the glare of the inn's lantern, Gordon

Aboyne and his companion lurched out onto the frost speckled cobblestones. Supporting one another like a pair of gorillas, bellowing at the top of their voices bawdy verses of a sea shanty. The rascals headed in the direction of the church.

Barely through the gates, in sight of St Michael's, Mr Aboyne sunk to his knees exclaiming in a swash-buckling fashion: "Branwell, me hearty, me 'ed's a spinnin' like a top. I'm whirling about, whirling around. Save me from cracking my poor old skull upon yonder gravestones. Here, take my arm and haul me up, damn you."

"For England and Saint George – be gad, raise your longbows," cried young Brontë, himself losing balance and toppling over in an effort to lift his friend, collapsing in fits of laughter.

Mr Aboyne was about to reply in the words of Falstaff, who might as well have been their patron saint, whereupon his entire face froze, and for a while no sound escaped his lips.

"Hullo, what's that?" he said at length, his voice trembling. "Over there. Branwell, look... *The Bride*! I am on the verge of lunacy. First the automatic drawings in the sketch book, now this spectral visitation."

Branwell cast his gaze to the west, across the tombs dispersed with ornately decorated memorial tablets, crosses and angels. Sure enough, there was just enough light for him to make out a white-gowned figure, abstracted, the face seemingly mouldy and bloated. Yet in reality more the resemblance of a root vegetable – a large, hollowed-out, half cut swede or turnip. The very place she wandered being the fairly fresh plot of the unfortunate mill girl.

"Branwell, we must …"

"Mr Aboyne, I beg you concern yourself not so much with the supernormal… listen instead to the distinct notes of crackling twigs and leaves as she moves about."

Gordon pricked up his ears, drunk as he was, the feeling of euphoria had deserted him.

"Human then?"

"I believe so. Stay put, old fellow, and I'll sneak up to the house to fetch Father's flintlock. Tabby'll let me in round the back. I shan't be long, keep the bride under scrutiny. I'm going to approach round by the field. A surprise for our spectre I'll be bound. Wait for the signal."

"What signal? You're not going to shoot her, are you?" Gordon was horrified, fearing the gallows for both of them. "Put a ball through her?"

"In the air! In the air you dimwit. I'll fire into the heavens, then we grapple to the ground whoever is out there and apprehend them. Ghouls, spectres and hobgoblins be damned. Headless horsemen and will o' the wisps depart. This night is ours, Gordon, for England, for Saint George!"

Soon after, Young Brontë's bold initiative paid off. After the briefest of altercations, the mysterious intruder was led up to the east-facing house. Rev Brontë (alerted by gunfire) was perfectly placed to offer solace to the poor wounded bird that was escorted up the steps, the hour being nearly half past eleven.

Nothing much shocked him anymore, no judgement or criticism

seemed appropriate. The vicar got the gist of the night's events from Tabitha Aykroyd, responding in a dignified, helpful way.

"My dear Mrs Welland, come through to the kitchen. Tabby...?" he directed, "a jug of milky cocoa be required. Boil a pan."

"Ah, more smoke oop the chimbley," the servant cackled. "Coom in, ma'am, coom on in."

Her bridal gown much dirtied during the scuffle, holding a pulpy, warty mask, the woman meekly did as asked – her world collapsed, far beyond embarrassment for her bizarre actions that night.

"What are you lads hanging around for?" he scolded. "Up to bed, the pair of you, now. Place my pistol back in its case boy. I am personally taking charge and will make sure Mrs Welland occupies a sofa couch for the night. Are you quite well, my dear? I shall have a good fire banked up. Your ordeal appears remarkable."

"Thank you, Vicar. I am quite recovered. What I was doing in that churchyard, heaven only knows. I can only apologise."

"Hush, hush, now. Branwell, Mr Aboyne – our lips are sealed. Tomorrow morning, when Mrs Welland is rested, we shall discuss the matter further. Gracious, such a pistol crack. I was awoken, believing a murderer to be on the loose. My dear Mrs Welland, what must you think of members of my family?"

"Drawn to that poor mill girl's grave. Was it to empathise?" she wondered out loud. "But she be dead. Oh, Gordon and your son, once they realised it was I, of all people, lurking about in this silly bridal gown from the back of my cupboard under moth balls, behaved like perfect gentlemen. Sleepwalking – *a state of trance*, don't they call it?" No respite from her grief, she thought of the tea shop and dear Mr Trowbridge spilling crumbs down his front and nearly broke into sobs. She felt a black hole in her heart, a darkness swallowing her up that refused to lift.

"Quite so," answered the vicar brusquely. "Dr Otley shall be summoned first thing. You can depend on it."

Fifteen

Breakfasting on fresh bread and a dish of chocolate, Dr Otley first became alerted to the worrying predicament of Mrs Welland by an early visit from the Brontës housemaid. Thus, riding at a brisk trot, he arrived at Glebe House, welcomed warmly by the sisters.

But this was not a social call, and they were in the vicar's study where the walls (similar to his surgery) were tastefully painted in an off-white distemper. The elegant room furnished simply: cabinet piano, a small writing desk over by the casement window, chairs set about, a peat fire roaring - the practitioner was able to carry forth an examination of Mrs Welland, pronouncing her physically fit and none the worse for her exposure to the cold and damp from the previous night. Gentle probing on his part, for which the doctor's good looks and charm were well suited, brought forth a tearful account of her recent experience: the shock of coming across the open coffin at Oxenhope village and for this Dr Otley proved able to help in small measure.

"I am, this morning, riding that way to visit a patient and shall make *tactful* enquiries and report back to you, Mrs Welland. I'm quite sure the late Mr Trowbridge should approve – to discover the nature of his sudden demise, to ascertain the church at which he be buried. Why, you might think to visit his grave and place flowers after all. What harm be there expressing one's grief in an open way.

He was a bachelor, and you a respectable widow. You should only cause yourself added anxiety by denial. Death is a natural part of living. In time, you will get over your loss. Take the powders and tonic as prescribed. I shall visit you next week."

"Will I? Get over it I mean," she sighed. "I don't feel that way at present. My spirits at a low ebb and set to stay fixed I fear. But I am grateful Doctor. If Samuel you could but enquire of Mr Trowbridge, this will be of some comfort in my trials. I shall gather my things and depart shortly for my brother's house in Haworth. That is where I can be found this next fortnight. Allowing for Rev Patrick's blessing, I have instructed the sexton to burn my bridal gown and that turnip face upon his next bonfire."

"Very well. Expect me to call. Good day. Violet sends her love. She is over at Scrivelsby Hall attending to affairs, appointing a new estate manager."

"Send my love also."

Sixteen

With a bracing gallop, Dr Otley rode up a grassy slope, thence, his faithful horse cantered along a ridge following a rough moorland road allowing him to enjoy splendid views upon his descent into the village, where he arrived around midday. The weather had held off, no rain or sleet, but a glimmer of early spring sunshine peering through clouds.

Coming in the opposite direction on horseback from a large green surrounded by pretty stone walls and flag-roofed dwellings, a stout bewigged personage raised his wide-brimmed hat in greeting.

"Dr Otley, what a pleasure. I have not seen you since... when was it... last September over at Keighley. Your practice flourishes, I trust? Mine certainly does. My tincture lozenges are all the rage in these parts."

"Dr Greystoke, hello. I too am on my rounds – a Mr Trowbridge?" the physician queried, leaning forward to pat his dappled mare's mane."

"Indeed, I know to whom you refer. Set upon by ruffians. These days, even our villages can be unsafe. I treated his injuries."

"Although he died as a result of the attack. Recently buried, I hear."

"Otley, what are you rattling on about? *Burial*? Am I that much of a quack? The fellow's making a full recovery."

"Trowbridge? You're certain?"

"The same. Bruised head, ribs, grazes, concussion, twisted knee joint. No, I'd say he's a game sort, getting on a bit, but I'm pleased to say that he's on the mend."

"Blazes man, I have it on good authority, an eyewitness, that he is recently deceased. How can this be Dr Greystoke? Unless the surnames of two individuals be the same, am I close? This must be the solution."

"Not quite, but a guinea if you can answer correctly," the other grinned, but still gave nothing away.

"Tell me," Asked Dr Otley exasperated, fuming and indignant. "Is the damnable Trowbridge alive or dead?"

"Very well, Otley – both DEAD AND ALIVE."

"What? How come?"

"Twins, *twin brothers* involved, you oaf. Marmaduke Trowbridge was indeed buried last week after a bout of pneumonia. He suffered much of last month with weak lungs, susceptible to infection. The brothers, who have both resided in Oxenhope, are estranged, bitterly so, due to an imbalance of inheritance – barely spoke to one another in the last decade. Edwin, a retired engineer, the pleasanter of the pair, my profitable patient whom I attend, is to be found convalescing at his house on the outskirts of the village. Bandaged up, but alive."

"Well this intelligence is bound to lift the heart of one dear to me. What wonderful news. You are to become the recipient of a brace of pheasants, duck and champagne from a certain Mrs Welland. Doctor, whereabouts can I find this Edwin Trowbridge? I pray in earnest he be the person I seek."

"Crummack Crag House," came the answer, gifted by his amused companion. "Past the village store and postal office then upon the left."

Thus, it came to pass a fortnight hence, romance again blossomed in the tea shop at Oxenhope. The pair of turtle doves had only eyes for each other. Mrs Welland and her beau, the elderly Edwin Trowbridge, slipped back into gear. A small, velvet box with a jeweller's crest in silver foil stamped upon the lid, was shyly passed by the retired engineer over a plate of Bakewell tarts, signifying an engagement in the offing - an engagement which was duly accepted with a smile.

"Well, that's wonderful Mr Trowbridge." The widow smiled, placing the ring on her finger, examining the gold band and rose cluster of precious stones with approval, "wonderful."

Seventeen

Emily Brontë sat perched on a piano stool in front of the keyboard with its vertically arranged strings - a Chopin sonata, the finely played *Scherzo: Molto vivace*, echoed into the hall, filling the parsonage with music. The music appreciated much by Charlotte and Anne, busy putting final flourishes to a set of watercolours at the dining room table. Being early March, fires were lit in all the downstairs rooms, dinner being prepared by Tabitha, the smell of roasting meat and Yorkshire pudding wafting from the kitchen. So presently (at least) all was well and good.

Suddenly the front door opened. The Rev Patrick Brontë stood sternly inside the porch, first thumping his riding boots on the mat, thence shaking rainwater off his coat and clerical hat before entering the hall. Charlotte and Anne hurried to greet him. His mood was perplexed, the sound of the tinkling piano from the study softened him somewhat.

"Poor, poor Tilly Craddon from the milliner's shop," he sighed, being helped off with his heavy black coat, the front door shut against the bitter draught. "My dears, she has run away. Her father the tobacconist is worried. Mrs Craddon, after all she has done for her fallen daughter these past months, is in total despair. The matter is doubly disturbing."

"How come, Papa?" asked Anne, brushing off the vicar's hat.

"Common knowledge, Tilly, such a decent, lovable young lady

endured a stillbirth, while out of wedlock. Although praise be she survived, remaining in good health after the labour. She is but seventeen years old and has left the cottage without saying a word to her parents. Gone off without a by-your-leave, taking the little body of her dead son with her. Her parents, Frederick and Petunia, have shown such patience and compassion throughout the crisis. Her fall from grace is a matter of much continued speculation."

"Yet, Papa," cautioned Anne, "Miss Craddon must herself be distressed. You must allow for her traumatised feelings."

The Rev Brontë was hardly listening, still more turbulent waters must be negotiated.

"She has quit the cottage, her home, and worse, taken the body of the child. Where to, none of us know... Branwell!" he thundered up the staircase. "Branwell, where are you, you layabout?"

Silence.

"At this hour," commented Charlotte dryly, "The snug at the Black Bull, downing a quart of gin, else brandy."

"If he is the father then that is the absolute end. If he sired Tilly's child God help me, I'll ..."

"Take care. I have never once heard brother Branwell talk or make mention of Tilly Craddon, whether under the influence of alcohol or not, Papa."

"No, Charlotte, but an insidious rumour has been circulating about town for some time, that my own boy has fathered a child. Not through marriage, but by casual acquaintance, leading a young woman on. Drunkard or not, by heavens, if I manage to wring the truth from him and he is responsible for Miss Craddon's situation I shall see to it that he honours his obligations."

"Yet where has Tilly gone, Papa? Perhaps actually to seek out the true father? Has she wandered over the moors to Keighley or to Hebden Bridge?"

"At this time of year, even on the cusp of spring, the Pennines are treacherous. The weather is so unpredictable. Let us pray she has sought out a sympathetic party closer to home here in town and will return to her loving parents shortly. She is such a decent and hard working girl for this to have happened to."

"Enough rumour and speculation. A good dinner awaits Father, a chance to chat about more pleasant things. Dr Otley and Violet Kenyon remain a true partnership, she now living at Scrivelsby Hall of late."

"Indeed. Well, dear old Kenyon has much to be pleased about, and deservedly so."

Eighteen

That most worthy and brave individual, Captain Charles Atwell. A pugilist, a swordsman and a hero, was moved to act.

Engaged on an errand (the son of Brigadier Sir Damian Laurence) had travelled specially by coach from his attractive house, one of those notable dwellings that exist rising in successive tiers from the shore at Scarborough. He was not on an errand of military intelligence as such, but rather of the heart, of two hearts he supposed. His adorable Tilly, the girl he knew only by her Christian name whom he had met quite by chance about the esplanade and taken to tea the previous summer. Whose parents' names were Fred and Petunia, or some such, and that he had last seen in ebullient spirits departing The Bell, the coaching inn, amid much happy waving and promises of a letter… which never materialised.

That playful beauty, of straw-coloured hair, short of stature, attractive and broad-shouldered Tilly had been on holiday at the marine spa. The captain was smitten. Over the coming days, they had scarcely been apart and had been chaperoned (not too suffocatingly) by her amused parents. They visited the spa, the Rotunda Museum, the castle up on the headland, the assembly rooms, the orchestra and concerts. Mrs Craddon had recorded, before setting out on the mail coach, his address in her pocketbook - Tilly, herself, accepted a silver, engraved ring from her captain as a keepsake. There should have been but a short delay until nuptials were announced. All parties had dearly wished for this outcome. What then had happened since?

A soldier at Waterloo, who served in close proximity to the Duke, himself a captain, was not to be put off, his honourable intentions brought to nought. Haworth, the mill town on the edge of the Pennines he knew for certain was the lass's hometown. Haworth was where he headed. And yet as he took lodgings at the respectable Kings Arms, as opposed to the loutish Black Bull tavern at the top of the cobbled street, the future already seemed somewhat shaky and insecure.

Of all the circumstances to blight a romantic fellow's pilgrimage on behalf of cupid, no sooner did he disembark from the stagecoach, exuberant in his quest, seeing everything about the smoky mill town in a positive light, halfway up the fearfully steep hill he enquired of a decent gentlewoman might she know of a certain Tilly. Thereafter, he was answered, in glowing terms, that the lady believed a Tilly worked at the milliners shop a little further up and not too far out of his way.

A uniformed, gallant officer for Queen and country, though burdened down with baggage, duly enquired at the front counter, only to be singularly rebuffed. He was promptly informed by a somewhat pompous proprietor that Tilly no longer was in her employment, had become 'indisposed' and would not be returning to her post. No other details were forthcoming, and his enquiry was abruptly shut down with a 'Good day, sir'.

Making his apologies for troubling the madam, the captain found himself once more out on the cobbles, stumbling up the steep street of millworker cottages and shops, none the wiser, in search of the recommended hostel.

'Indisposed', what was that supposed to mean?' He thought.

Nineteen

At the parsonage there had been a tumultuous row that night.

After his late return to Glebe House, after another evening at the Black Bull Branwell was shocked to receive (for the first time in ages) a severe reprimand from his father. Here, in front of his sisters, to be snatched by the earlobe and dragged like a naughty school boy into the study. He, Branwell Brontë! Published in the poetry column of *The Halifax Journal*, accused (wrongly accused) by father of putting a bun in the oven of some shop girl he had never met. Granted, he was aware of a scurrilous rumour circulating. No truth in it... although admittedly a matter amongst drinking pals to be foolishly boasted about if a brandy fireball were in the offing.

Tonight down in the study however, his own dear papa, normally so good a judge of character and events, a rational and forgiving clergyman, open to the truth, had demanded that his errant son own up to having sired a child out of wedlock! Preposterous!! Once Branwell had fought his corner and sloped back upstairs in a huff to close his bedroom door, substance misuse was thankfully close to hand. He imbibed a dose of laudanum.

Lost in a druggy stupor, expectant of calming, languid visions of vast oriental temples, pagodas and palaces of unparalleled splendour and opulence, scintillating cultural life beyond even Ming,

Tang and Sung dynasties. Instead, the opiate turned against his better intelligence. Peering into space, something familiar started happening to the candlelit rooms' wallpaper - a shifting of mass, possibly to do with guilt, albeit unfounded guilt. The recent altercation downstairs affecting his mind, magnifying sins he had not even committed, magnifying themselves into a diabolical hallucination to behold. Babies faces began to appear among the floral patterns on the wallpaper, multiplying like pupae, one on top of another on top of another on top of another, to cover one entire wall... then another, then another and then the other.

Undulating, shivering, glistening chubby heads born of volcanic ooze. Scaly skinned with little oval, fanged mouths and black eyes. Wailing not for nourishment in the form of milk, but to be suckled on blood as does the leech in the swamplands of America.

After not too long Branwell could bare this increase of hellish, bulbous-browed infants no more, nor their incessant crying.

He jumped out of bed wearing a nightshirt and cap, fumbling by candlelight towards the window. He heaved the frame upward, eager to breathe in the fresh night air, purge his head of infernal wallpaper babies crying for his attention.

During this desperate effort to clear his mind however, in a more sober judgement, his eye became distracted by someone down on the church path - a stooping figure wearing a shawl and pushing a handcart. He was to puzzle over this ceaselessly for the remainder of the night, until dawn's final glimmer and cock crow.

Around noon the following day, the weather bright and chilly crisp, dazzled by the strong sunshine blazing in from the window, John Brown the official Parish sexton, stumped into the Rev Brontë's study bowler hat in hand, gaiters and hobnail boots cleaned of cloying mud. The vicar was sat upright at his study table composing a sermon.

"John, my dear fellow," said he, still writing. "Would you take a dish of tea?"

"I will."

"You have the funerals of old Miss Shellibar and Tadworth brothers' sister, Matilda, in hand I trust? I made arrangements. They are to be buried at ten and half past one tomorrow respectively. Lucy Brock is on Friday at two. You told me our churchyard is becoming increasingly overcrowded, but folk do still continue to be determined to find their last resting place high up here on the valley slope. Alas, in Haworth the mortality rate seems fierce, room is becoming scarce."

"The flat headstone slabs might be slid across and soil removed to accommodate the poorer mill folk. Ten foot down and more on top like a layer cake is the norm. Mingling with the bones of our forebears." Put in John, matter of factly.

"How is Martha and your dear wife John? I trust Charlotte's home-made jam and pickle was appreciated?"

"They are well, Vicar. Might I amuse you over tea with an interesting item of news? Hello Tabitha," he said grinning, as the house servant brought in a tray.

"Dear boy, anything of interest in this bleak, lonely parish is worth expressing. I am all ears."

"Well Padre, I have it on good authority from Mr Vernon, the sexton out at Stanbury, and Mr Healey at Oxenhope, that a number of graves have been disturbed recently. With corpses being vacated from the churchyards."

"Hmm... what else can we suppose of such desecration than that a gang of resurrectionists is at work. Illicit cadavers supplied to the surgeons at the teaching hospitals. I dread to think, but the amount of bodies these woeful men succeed in uprooting every year in the country, let alone Londinium, may be worse than feared."

"P'raps, though I must add that these be the bodies of infants - four altogether. Mr Vernon is insistent that the clergy around here be alerted. I will myself keep a vigil this night in the hope of catching these people, get them afore a Justice of the Peace. Mr Todge be of a like mind. The graves of children and babies is surely and without a doubt sacrosanct."

"Commendable. A rotation of duty is advisable. Gracious heavens John, at least Haworth kirkyard has so far been spared the wicked pick and shovel of the resurrection men."

Branwell was passing the open study door with a cup of chocolate in hand when he overheard the gist of the conversation. He popped his head round putting forth some useful intelligence.

"Papa," said he, observing an altogether warmer and more affectionate look in his father's eye towards him, "I beg you and John come outside and accompany me along the church path, for if my surmise be correct, I fear us at Haworth *have not been spared on this occasion*. Bring a spade, Mr Brown, sir, we shall have need of such a tool."

How incongruous that upon a sunny, vibrant Tuesday afternoon the churchyard in daylight looking well-maintained, that three men should be presently gathered round peering into the hollow of a small, empty white coffin propped on top of a heap of clay.

"I confess, before we took it upon ourselves to dig down and check the coffin, there was barely enough disturbance of earth to determine anything amiss. Whoever did this took care to neatly replace the soil afterwards. Had Branwell not made a point of us inspecting the infant's burial area, I should have noticed nothing amiss," said the vicar scratching his head.

"Me neither," admitted the sexton with a shrug, leaning on his spade heavily. "We do have a missing corpse of a child, though. Interred last September. The grave depth be shallower and easy to excavate."

"Despicable," exclaimed the Rev Bronte. "The child's body should not even be fresh. What price should they attain for one decomposing?"

Silence for a short while. Until broken by John Brown.

"Come on Branwell, don't just stand there like an oaf, speak up lad. What have we missed?"

"Last night flinging wide the bedroom window, I saw a woman with a headscarf hurrying from this very spot. She wore a shawl."

"A female? Why, that is astounding," sighed the Rev Brontë, wanting to get back indoors. "There's something very darkly odd about all of this."

"Summit very queer indeed for sure," added the sexton. He put on his bowler hat, strong jaw tensed, chin jutting out in defiant disgust..

Twenty

Dr Otley was hastening down Main Street, after visiting the apothecary shop, when he caught sight of a familiar set of shoulders. A certain distinctive strut that instantly reminded him of an old school friend from way back.

"Charles… is that you?" he bellowed. "Apologies if I be mistaken, sir. Are you bound for Flora's tuck shop? Or a French lesson with Miss Prudence, the gloriously bosomed teacher? State your business my old friend." said he smiling broadly.

Lively laughter followed by an embrace of old scholars, was a precursor for a visit to the best tea shop in town. The chance meeting sparking off like a Roman candle, an exchange of fond memories, hilarious episodes concerning the pair's school life, but that was not all…

"An officer in the Lifeguards Regiment, your crimson and gold uniform suits. How is your dear father, busy at soldiering? I recall those Fortnum hampers he sent you."

"He was ill with gout recently. Still the old stiff upper lip of course. Still lives north of the border."

"But what in God's name brings you to Haworth of all places? Last I heard, you were nicely set up in Scarborough."

"I am."

"Were you not to marry the Lady McFane of Dalkeith, daughter of the Duke of Buccleugh, the Scotch heiress?"

"Failed, fell through it did, and for that I'm grateful. Josephine and I were never really compatible. A mutual parting. Thankfully, we shared the same sense of the ridiculous in regard to the 'arranged' marriage expectation. Mother was terribly disappointed, but what can one do? Live a lie, a pretence? Blazes, she will be ever more disappointed when I inform her that I am seeking the hand of a shop girl. It will probably kill her... and father."

The doctor laughed uproariously, tears of mirth streaming down his cheeks. "Then, who, pray, is this lovely lady? Forgive my brevity, I always recall you never liked to conform."

"I'm not really that bothered if I'm to marry beneath me. What about you, Sam?"

"I can't talk. My own sweetheart is pregnant with child. Violet is expecting, the baby due shortly. We personally couldn't be happier. Alas, she is a married woman, or rather, legally tied. I am the father. Our baby could affect her entitlements to the mill owner Sir James Grueldyke's, lands and estates."

"So, what does Sir James himself have to say, or is he being kept in the dark about the true origins of the pregnancy? If there is a duel to be had, I can act as your second."

"He was murdered last year."

"I see. Well, what lads we are. I am to marry beneath me and you, Dr Otley, seek a woman above your station. Shall we toast?"

"But you haven't answered my question Charles. Who, I say, is your lucky intended?"

"Her first name I know for certain to be Tilly. She is, or rather *was*, according to my research, employed at the milliner's shop across the road. I confess, I have so far been unable as yet to seek out her home address. I must speak to her and her parents urgently."

"A squat girl, heavily bosomed with broad shoulders, straw-blonde hair - a very attractive counter assistant. Violet buys her hat creations from over the way."

"You have her description exactly Sam. I met her while she holidayed in Scarborough, but for reasons unknown, a vital letter has not been forthcoming. I am determined to claim her for my own, come what may."

Dr Otley lost all humour from his face. He appeared dour and professional, as though addressing a terminal patient.

"My dear sir, prepare yourself for a bomb blast worse than any you fought to avoid at Waterloo."

"That bad? What, how come? For God's sake explain yourself Samuel."

"I will be blunt and to the point. I know she ran away. Miss Craddon, this girl you seek, gave birth to a stillborn. The father, I am told by Dr Edgar in confidence is in all likelihood a brute of an agricultural labourer who forced himself upon her down an alley as she made her way home. A rumour persists that a local poet and lounger, Branwell Brontë, might have been responsible, but I dismiss that with a pinch of salt."

"Oh. My silly, silly mouse," said the captain, pushing away his cake plate. "If only I had known of this sooner, she and her parents could have stayed at my house in Scarborough. Damn convention, damn society and the way individuals are forced to behave and think. Tilly was forced by her circumstances to erase me from the equation, fearing rejection, pompous platitudes if she wrote. As though I, who have seen so much blood and carnage, torment and the sharp end of life, cared a jot. Raped by a blaggard. Good god. She deserved open arms, promises of devotion. By now, the crisis passed, she should be concerned with happier things – our life together ..."

"Well, Charles, these are brave words indeed. Let us be glad that you are billeted in Haworth. A search of the town has proved utterly fruitless. Frederick, the girl's father, and his wife are at their wits ends."

"Pray Tilly has not harmed herself, consumed with misery, decided to end her own life."

"Let us keep faith, Charles. Violet is always telling me to make the best of situations and not to brood upon the worst outcome. That will not do. Now, sir, you must put that military strategist's brain of yours to good account. Think, like on a battlefield, what are your options? What is the likeliest places Miss Craddon may be found, given the circumstances? Dammit, man the moors, or another town perhaps, or a hamlet in the Worth valley. A fortnight has passed and still no word. Time is of the essence. At least the weather is warmer."

"Then, Sam, I launch my campaign to rescue the one I love."

"Bravo!" The friends clinked teacups hard enough to resonate across the tea room, receiving a disapproving look from the owner in response to their improper use of bone China..

Twenty One

That night Violet Kenyon went into labour. She was attended by Sir Giles Stamford, a surgeon of prestige from York. Mr Kenyon the architect insisted that Dr Otley take a back seat on this occasion. This allowed the birthing to proceed uncomplicated by Samuel's presence. He and Mr Kenyon should remain downstairs, a tradition amongst gentlemen, on tenterhooks sipping port and smoking cigars, awaiting the nurse's call.

Everything that could be done was done. The staff at Scrivelsby Hall, everyone of them, wished only well for their mistress and that the child be delivered into this world safely.

Around teatime the wind increased, and the rain pattered the windows. Now the wind surged with vehemence, howling into the dip, battering the old manor house, shaking the tiles and chimney pots.

Twenty Two

Meanwhile in Haworth outside the Kings Arms at the top of Main Street, Captain Atwell buttoned his topcoat, secured his sabre, and mounted a hired black steed of sleek proportions. The young, frisky animal, bred for speed, which the landlord had procured from Mr Stafford. The wild-eyed beast snorted, but sensing its rider could be equally wilful and reckless, settled nicely into a companionable trot. It had been raining earlier, and a breeze started up. The landlord warned of an incoming storm and to wrap up well.

'A soldier's instinct is important,' Charles told himself. His little mouse was up there somewhere. "I know it. So help me, I shall find her or die in the attempt," he chuckled, full of bravado.

"Where are you Tilly, my little mouse?" the captain shouted, his voice competing with the violence of the storm. Wind and rain lashing against his face, fork lightning to the west, the storm moving closer as measured by the time taken for the resonance of rumbling thunder to reach his position after strikes. By instinct and process of location elimination, he made haste for a stone circle marked on the map lent to him by the doctor.

These monuments would provide shelter he surmised. So far, no habitation he had visited had any notion of seeing a young, abandoned woman roaming the vicinity. Thus, he proceeded to ride his steed (who obviously knew the Pennine landscape better than he) along a poorly maintained cart track until he approached a hillock and spied a single lantern, the light flickering, but distinctive. Filled with renewed hope, he took encouragement, kicking his spurs into the shiny flanks of the horse.

Jumping down and patting the animal, he proceeded up the peaty, heather-tufted hillock by foot.

"Who be there?" he called.

Surmounting the rise, half prepared to encounter a skin-clad barbarian to behold him wielding a stone axe, the area (he knew from guidebooks) steeped in pagan legend.

One of the stones laid flat and central to the rest conjured up an altar for sacrificial purposes. But the light afforded from this vantage by the oil lamp revealed not merely a configuration of jagged stones, but a definite circle of six tiny bundles wrapped in cloth, spread evenly apart.

Approaching one of them, he was taken aback, for the exposed, wrinkly face alerted the captain to the grim reality that these were dead children. The infants were organised in a ceremonial fashion.

Huddled beside a rock was a grubby woman, a handcart nearby. She was filthily clad in skirts and a shawl, peering with gleaming eyes into space, her lips silently murmuring.

Given his close proximity, she appeared not to have become aware of his presence. The captain felt a great sadness descend upon him, for both the bedraggled woman up here alone, and the swaddled dead laid out on the grass in a circle before him.

A boom of thunder rippled across the sky above as lightning lit up the area allowing every detail of the surroundings to be made clear and succinct.

Charles, in that piercing, boldly lit second, realised that it was Miss Craddon sat sobbing, disarranged, clothes stained and torn.

"I have saved the little ones. Saved them from the grave. They will thrive up here, I know it," she gasped.

Twenty Three

Whilst this storm raged across the moors and much of the north, Scrivelsby Hall was being buffeted and shaken, the knotted timbers of such an old house more than used to countless bombardments by nature.

Mr Kenyon and Dr Otley sat in oak Tudor armchairs either side of the immense stone hearth listening with mounting concern as the surgeon offered his latest prognosis of Violet's present condition.

"I fear there is every chance that I may save the baby Otley. Alas, the mother herself will not likely survive. The birth is proving difficult due to a breach of the womb. Violet is failing fast and her constitution will not be able to withstand, nay survive, the immense blood loss. We are thus at a sadly critical juncture. I must return upstairs. I am so sorry to be the bearer of such tragic news."

Twenty Four

"Tilly, come away now, come." The captain guided the dazed girl through the swirling rain (quickly past the flat altar stone, casting a 'bombastic side eye' in its direction) only to become witness to a truly startling event.

***

A deafening explosion and crack of thunder dominated all of his senses as a crackle of lightning zig-zagged from the clouds, striking the hill top, connecting directly with one of the swaddled bundles, igniting it into flame.

Helpless to the events unfolding before him, the captain watched agog as a chain reaction took place.

A static blue charge moved in a considered arc (pausing at times as if to be making conscious decisions) to each of the other five bundles, one, by one, by one. Until all six were aflame in the round.

In a moment, the electromagnetic energy was gone.

Struck dumb by the combination of noise, light and confusing events, Captain Atwell had not noticed a sudden transformation to Tilly's demeanour as she was in his arms.

The woman that she was before had re-emerged, eyes focused, bright once more, soul restored.

Recognition followed. "What… what am I doing here? Why are

we here in the dark?" she quizzed, "Charles, is it really you, darling? What has happened here? Hold me close."

The rain abated; the storm appeared to settle.

Twenty Five

Scrivelsby Hall was in uproar. A momentous, joyous occasion, for at the very moment the storm had reached its zenith, a vivid streak of fork lightning struck somewhere to the east (witnessed by many as a *portent,* an omen) and Violet Kenyon rallied, displaying untold reserves of inner strength.

Consequently, both mother and baby were in fine fettle after the ordeal, that seemed at one stage so close to ending her life.

The surgeon was astounded, the midwife had never seen anything so remarkable. Sir Giles had recently departed in his carriage glad that the storm had blown itself out, making his journey home much more tolerable.

The architect Mr Kenyon, and Dr Samuel Otley were taking a glass of Champagne when three rapid knocks at the living room door announced visitors.

The housekeeper allowed a moment to compose herself. "Forgive me, sir, an acquaintance of yours I believe. A Captain Atwell, a very fine if damp-looking, gen-tleman officer, and a traumatised looking lady, all drenched through after being caught out in the storm, begging shelter for the night. I must procure hot water. The gentleman can have a hip bath in the kitchen, the lady upstairs. Covered in mud kicked up off the road in that awful weather."

Twenty Six

*T*he air seemed to shudder. Charlotte, awakened by an intensely unpleasant sensation of being observed, peering into the gloom of her parsonage bedroom, was surprised to find her literary hero, Lord Byron, looking down directly at her.

Yet the poet, author of Don Juan, died in Greece, in 1824. The body embalmed, secured in a tin coffin and stowed aboard a ship bound for England, thence the family vault at Hucknall Torkard. She knew all this – without any shadow of a doubt...

Three weeks earlier

Dr Otley pulled on the reins of his horse, trotting over towards a familiar landmark... standing stones upon the hillock that broke the green swell of the moors.

The location of the great lightning strike that took place some months back. An event noted by the local smallholders who work isolated farmsteads hereabouts, as a forewarning of menace.

Lightning had been known to set fires raging across the moors in summer, but this meteorological event was notable for the precise nature of the strike. Heather and wild grass about the monoliths being blackened, scorched.

A number of individuals were presently gathered, ruminating upon a certain recent archaeological discovery.

"A most agreeable enterprise." One man was heard to say, scrutinizing the ground before him, "The acidity of peat, the tannin, the dearth of oxygen means that even a cabbage leaf might last for several thousand years in this ground."

"Hence, this carcass has survived. I should judge him Palaeolithic – what say you, Sir Fenton?" Put in another, down on his knees, small shovel in hand.

"Bronze Age possibly. We must remove him to carry out a proper examination. Lord Edmonton our worthy patron has determined it thus. Ah, Dr Otley, please step over here. Our archaeological dig began some time back by members of the Haworth Society, of which your father-in-law Mr Kenyon is a subscriber. Rev Patrick Brontë our chairperson. Not only have we unearthed some interesting pottery shards, but a most extraordinary find indeed. Our amateur fraternity is reeling, this be so utterly unexpected."

Moving forward, the doctor, himself well acquainted with the five persons (mostly gentry, that is Sir Fenton, Mr Clarke, Mr Clough, John Martin and Mr Frank Bishop) knelt at the side of the open trench gazing wondrously upon the figure confined therein.

"Twas only that lightning strike that stirred our interest," said a member of the team.

Seen within was a curled, leathery body, pinioned down by three iron rods – pierced through the spleen, the heart and the forehead.

The simian face appeared at rest, although a rictus grin, lips drawn back, revealed a mouth possessing a pair of barbed fangs on the upper quadrant perfectly preserved. A disturbing image.

"All 'up in the air' at present Otley. We need to take stock of this specimen. Lord Edmonton, the patron of the Archaeological Society, insists that the carcass is best removed to his home Oakley House, at the earliest opportunity."

"To preserve it you must keep the body pliable and moist," the doctor suggested, seeing various carriages presently down in the dip. Notably, a stout rural wagonette, procured in readiness for the transit of the unearthed specimen to its new home.

"Well, Doctor, we are but a gathering of enthusiastic amateurs. Lord Edmonton, is the only true antiquarian among us."

"Nonetheless, your perseverance over the years investigating historical sites has paid off at last. I rejoice that you have now discovered something of real note."

"We were alerted to the stones by the publicity of the lightning strike during that great storm. It has long been a rumour that this area was once a megalithic temple. There may be a pattern of trenches, further burials, who knows?"

"Gentlemen… the peat man's removal is close at hand," Sir Fenton reminded his team, snatching up his trowel and cleaning the blade while the others were moved to act.

"The iron rods. Why are they employed to pinion a presumably dead body?" Asked the medical practitioner.

"Religious significance?" proposed Mr Martin.

"A sacrifice?" answered Frank Bishop.

"My own view relates that the rods were used as a form of grisly execution. The means to silence a convicted criminal, a perpetrator of a terrible crime," said Mr Clough.

"All of this is theoretical my dear Doctor," insisted Sir Fenton. "Let us run tests and await results. Lord Edmonton has a number of qualified professors, all eminent antiquarians expected from York soon to assist in analysing the remains. This dig shall be written up in our monthly journal. Mr Clarke being our secretary and chief scribe."

Frank bishop stood proud, arms folded, surveying the well-executed investigation "Wait till the *Halifax Messenger* gets wind of this, or better still the London papers!"

"I believe Lord Edmonton wishes for our discovery to remain strictly amongst ourselves for now."

"Of course. At least until we have had a chance to publish our findings," the other conceded.

More activity ensued around the trench. Dr Otley leant against a huge boulder to smoke a cigar, watching the peculiar iron rods being prised one by one from the leathery body. To be placed aside, catalogued and tagged. Thence the ape-man, wrapped in a canvas tarpaulin, was carefully purveyed to its waiting means of transport.

Fig 3

Twenty Seven

Relinquishing a period of lurching from one crisis to another Branwell Brontë (indefatigable wit, poet, wild card, painter, cartoonist) at last found a wholesome distraction from imbibing copious drink and opiates. A woman of high birth, who attended church and occasionally accompanied his father on visits to the poor of Haworth.

She was the Lady Lysander of Oakley House, the wife of Lord Edmonton.

A strong intellect, a quick mind and great beauty, both fashionable and fickle, she craved company and excitement. For (unhappily, by way of an arranged marriage) she had ended up wed to an unromantic, aged Yorkshireman who knew little of women.

A taciturn individual, an antiquarian and scholar more given to his library, committed since youth to gain both alchemical and scientific knowledge, rather than understanding the intricacies of a relationship. An understanding that Branwell, a devilishly handsome cad, was much more suited.

Why else, for the last month, his heart pounding, did young Brontë, at the drop of a hat, ride like the devil across the moor to Oakley House, invited as a guest for afternoon tea, to serve as a means of amusement for Her Ladyship.

She herself possessed no real designs upon him as such. Although Branwell, with typical young male bravado, deemed otherwise and held out hopes for an elopement - constantly marvelling in disbelief at how the Lady Lysander (so lively and effervescent) could stand the company of that morose, old dwarf she chose to call her husband.

This was how he came to find himself close to the unfolding events regarding the prehistoric man.

For that same afternoon while reciting a popular poem by Walter Scott ('The Lay of the Last Minstrel'), perched upon the edge of the sofa, not as close to the Lady Lysander as he wished, the lovestruck fellow happened to glance out of the window when a creaky wagonette drew up to the main portico. A sheeted stretcher was unloaded, conveyed by Mr Clarke and Sir Fenton through the front doors of the half-timbered country house, then off to some distant chamber.

The Lady Lysander cared little for her elderly husband's affairs, promptly insisting Branwell accompany her at the piano to perform a duet. Branwell however, remained curious.

Not long after dutifully bowing as Lord Edmonton flanked by servants, entered the sitting room, begging his wife remain seated. Hunched over, leaning on a knobbly ash stick, the plain looking nobleman leered at his wife. "Lysander my dear, I put it to you we shall open a sanatorium that may house six to a dozen beds for the poor, allowing us to fulfil our Christian obligations. You have been known to witness squalor, attending the sick in the poorer parts of Haworth, along with the Rev Brontë and his daughters. I have long thought that commendable in one so young. We shall thus raise the bar. I give over part of my house to become a fresh-air sanatorium for the care of those poor townsfolk prone to tubercular disease of the lungs."

"Where in the house?" enquired Lady Lysander.

"Utilising the conservatory. I am instructing Baines to carry out the refurbishment. Twelve beds, and patients shall be installed within the week."

"'Poor visiting is one thing, but this... well, My Lordship's enterprise frankly astounds," she answered.

"Employ your fripperies to good effect. Take great pride that we, the Edmonton's, are committed to help those less fortunate, the denizens of mill workers slums. Why, you complain often enough about a lack of society to occupy your head. Now I present you with a worthwhile cause in which to become involved."

"Disease does not merely affect the undeserving poor - a gentleman, or a lady, of means may too fall victim," pointed out Branwell. Recalling his own precarious state of health and the fact that his elder sisters, Maria and Elizabeth, both died of consumption back in 1825.

"Though, your papa, a staunch Tory, a ceaseless campaigner for improved sanitation, cannot, I'll wager, fail to be impressed by my scheme. Why, I'd say the West Lane Baptist Chapel, the local Methodists, churchmen and dissenters alike, will applaud my good works – open to it – practical Christianity in action. More than mere words, but deeds!"

"You speak, sir, as though like Saint Paul at Damascus. You've undergone a deeply meant conversion, but pray, might you take a moment to consider the grave risk to your own health and that of your wife presented by housing infected patients so close to home?" the young man enquired, with the Lady Lysander's best interests at heart.

"Pennine air, fresh air, not the tainted air of a city's industrial fumes. I am a convert - my wife became one also. Ah, but tea is about to be served. I leave you, Lysander, in the no doubt pleasant and honourable company of young Branwell here. I must away upstairs to the library, in lieu of much study upon pressing antiquarian issues. I shall not be down to dinner."

"Before you leave to attend your scholarship, I must say sir, I applaud your bold initiative. An unprecedented act of benevolence on the part of the aristocracy for which my father shall be pleased beyond measure."

Branwell, about to resume the piano was not above ingratiating himself. "Might I beg to enquire of the sheeted stretcher unloaded from the wagonette?"

"You may not," came the firm answer. "That is a private matter beholden to the Haworth Archaeological Society."

Lord Edmonton was as good as his word. The Lady Lysander, upon a further visit, informed Branwell that she never once heard her husband mention Christianity, else 'good works', prior to this sanatorium idea.

Twenty Eight

A number of professors from York, and their orderlies, had since arrived to stay at the country house.

Baines and a host of servants cleared out, then repainted the conservatory. A dozen sick beds were installed. Dr Otley had himself recommended several patients with respiratory disease (including children) who would definitely benefit from nursing and better nourishment. *Phthisis*, or consumption, was a disease of the lungs and these twelve paupers of Haworth, at the beginning stages of the illness, made ideal candidates.

The Lady Lysander, upon her visits to the open windowed conservatory, always made sure she wore a hanky saturated in cologne over her face for protection. Her husband, Lord Edmonton, for all his pompous rhetoric, his praise of fresh air, kept well away. Never once visiting the patients, nor enquiring after their well-being.

The eminent professors from York, however, appeared to be genuinely involved, doing their rounds morning and noon, leaving the orderlies to the day to day care of patients.

A fortnight into the scheme it so happened the Lady Lysander confided to her young admirer, that a troubling issue had arose on one of her visits to the sanatorium. An issue she could not yet free from her mind.

Brontë, introducing a volume of poetry, was interrupted with a wave of her hand.

"I shall Your Ladyship, recite this afternoon a poem dear to both our hearts, taken from the quarto volume of the collected works of William Wordsworth, published in 1815, *The White Doe of Rylstone*, I begin by ..."

"No Branwell, pause awhile before continuing the verse. Poor dear Mr Sidley, what is to be done? Oh, it's really too disagreeable."

Closing the calf-bound volume, the young man checked his bookmark was in place. giving Her Ladyship his full, undivided attention.

"The weaver, Mr Sidley? The Newell Hill tenant?" he queried.

"A matter of some delicacy," she answered, a trite irritably. "Merely an observation, you understand, Branwell. In my privileged position, I feel it my duty to cheer up old Mrs Worth and visit the children in the sanatorium. Oh, and Elias Sidley, who is improving, or rather *was* improving, but now I find much reduced in both vigour and intellect."

"Really."

"So pale and listless. Even given his fragile condition, none of that chirpy, working-class humour one expects. Barely wakeful or conscious of my presence beside his bed. One of the professors, from York I believe, whilst attending to his rounds assured me Mr Sidley bore the symptoms of *encephalitis lethargica*, and that this would pass in a day or two."

"Elias Sidley?"

"Exactly so."

"Obviously you doubt the professor's prognosis. Another opinion can be obtained easily enough. Dr Otley, for instance, could ride over from his surgery in Haworth. I can call in on my way home."

"You misunderstand my concerns Branwell. I saw, with my own eyes, two distinct puncture wounds on Elias Sidley's neck. The orderly tried hurriedly to draw the collar of his nightshirt together, but I had already noted the marks. One assumes they to be bites from a fox, or a large feral cat roaming free in the grounds I know not which."

"Fangs!"

"Suppose a wild creature might have leapt upon the sill and crept in during the night. The glass windows to the conservatory are permanently left open."

"To allow for free circulation of air deemed beneficial for the consumptives. Yes, I know this. That would certainly make them vulnerable to such an attack from a prowling animal quick to pick up the scent. Although, surely, the patient would wake up and try to shake the thing off, alerting the orderlies. There would be a commotion, the incident would be reported."

"Yet Elias was not alone Branwell. His was not an isolated case, for I clearly saw young Freddie Hogg who grows ever stronger in my affections, normally so playful, attentive when I visit his bedside - bearing the marks of a beast upon his neck also."

Twenty Nine

The same night of his sister Charlotte's startling visitation of Lord Byron, it appeared that the homely parsonage situated at the top of the scarp (within easy reach of the moors) was prey to an unwanted intruder with peculiar affiliations.

Unable to sleep for pondering the intelligence gleaned to him that afternoon by Lady Lysander. A breeze rustling against the window alerted Branwell to a pale-faced individual with powdered hair, carrying a cocked hat, stood over by the door.

He couldn't subdue his excitement, for he recognised this fellow in knee breeches and silk stockings as William Wordsworth - most peculiarly a *young* Wordsworth - wasn't the man now in his late sixties? The poet, along with Lord Byron, had been a major influence on his own work. Branwell recalled how - expecting great things: praise, recommendation and ultimate fame - he submitted one of his own efforts for appraisal, sending it to Rydal Mount, the Wordsworth's home on the northern shore of Lake Windermere.

'The struggles of flesh and spirit' it was called, 'Scene 1 - Infancy'. A brilliant piece in his own view, only to receive no reply, no response to his letter, which galled him.

The Lakeland poet, a resident of Keswick, gazed benevolently upon the wanting acolyte's prone person. A thin, waspish smile appeared on his drawn lips, slightly parted revealing a pair of sharp fangs.

Branwell had imbibed neither laudanum nor hashish. Neglecting his cronies at the Black Bull, he had even relinquished those notorious *brandy fireballs*. Liquor was thus not coursing through his system. In plain words, he was sober as a judge, able to contemplate that the figure stood at the end of his bed was clearly no hallucination.

The fleshy exterior of Wordsworth wavered like the flame of a candle. For a time, the poet's features remained solid, the Wordsworth visage young Brontë recognised, began to slowly dissolve, to reveal the true being. A hideous, hairy, bandy-legged ape-like Palaeolithic - bearing those same gleaming fangs. Those, at least, were consistent.

"Who are you?" Croaked Branwell, reaching out to seize a water carafe to hurl. "I fear thee not, chameleon. Begone, lest I raise the house and have you caged behind bars. I shall not be hostage to an actor, a circus freak. Are you all smoke and mirrors? Speak up! You try my damned patience too far, sir."

"Very well," the other answered, not in grunts, but in a refined, well-spoken way. "I meant not to alarm thee, only to benefit us mutually. I have been raised from the peat by an old knight, so that I might walk forth again. I shall succour thee; mine own blood be thine blood."

"How speak you, a primitive, a cave dweller, in my own tongue with so much eloquence?"

"I absorb your culture, thy memory. I possess vast resources of knowledge. Hard to countenance I know. I walked with mammoths;

I saw pterodactyls swarm as ye see carrion crow. I am able to transform myself at will. What better than to change my appearance to that of a great English poet? To thereby appeal to your sensibilities faster. Chameleon is an apt description as any."

"The old knight you refer to is I presume, Lord Edmonton."

"Indeed, it is he who provides me with pauper livestock from which I feed, to gain strength after my lengthy incarceration below the ground. You see, I remain much weakened, as yet to attain my full potential, otherwise I should be addressing my young gentleman in the more pleasing aspect of William Wordsworth for longer."

"The fresh air sanatorium at Oakley House is a mere pretence then. I knew in my heart the old nobleman was up to something. All his talk of Christianity rung hollow."

"Christian, pagan - it matters not. I am an outcast to both. I yearn to instruct thee and thine to drink plentifully the sweetest liquor, to do and see untold things. Join me, Branwell Brontë, but first offer me thy neck. Step into the eternal nightworld and quit thy banal existence. Learn to sup. What image may I become to impress thee further. Coleridge, Lord Byron perhaps?"

"No! Begone you filthy leech."

"I am able to appease thy cravings. Become not my enemy."

"I shall gladly snatch up a sword to run you through, destroy your kind."

"The old knight's wife Lady Lysander is likely the cause of such unseemly bravado. She shall be mine own mate then."

The carafe of water flew across the room, but even before it crashed against the far wall, the space was empty.

The exasperated Branwell, alone to ponder his thoughts and take stock of the curious visitor, realised that the Lady Lysander must be protected, awakened to her husband's terrible deception.

Footsteps resonated on the landing, thereupon the bedroom door squeaked ajar. The Rev Patrick Brontë, adorned in a night cap, poked his head round, even with his poor eyesight able to take note of the spilt carafe.

"Are you alright, m'boy? I heard a noise," he asked, tentatively.

"Perfectly, father," the son lied, igniting a taper from the candle upon his beside cabinet, fully intending to smoke his clay pipe for a while. "Nothing to concern yourself over papa."

Fig 4

Thirty

At breakfast the following morning, Charlotte made mention of her encounter with Lord Byron. Whether a dream or visitation, she was uncertain. Even now, with the summer sun pouring through the windows, the boisterous prattle of her siblings filling the parlour. Branwell munched on his buttered toast and kept council.

Emily, however, who had been reading *Frankenstein*, by Mary Shelley, borrowed from the travelling library, pointed out it was Lord Byron who first helped bring about the writing when he and his travelling companion, John William Polidori, stayed at the villa Diodati with Mary and her partner, Percy Shelley, the poet. One night, a storm raging over the alps, Byron suggested they each write a ghost story.

The Fifth Baron and Percy Shelley had soon abandoned their efforts, but Polidori, himself an aspiring writer, and Mary Wolstencroft conceived the germ of ideas that should eventually lead to *Frankenstein* upon the one hand and *The Vampyre* on the other.

"But Polidori was not the first to write of vampyres. Joseph Sheridan Le Fanu, the Irish writer, brilliantly employs this fixation for another's blood in his novel *Carmillia*, a female of the type which I found quite admirable," enjoined Anne, reaching over for the butter dish.

"I am myself rather partial to Horace Walpole's *The Castle of Otranto*," the brother said, languidly sipping his coffee. He remained calm enough on the outside, but his inner self grew in turmoil.

Branwell must at all costs, alert Dr Otley that morning and share his experience. The Lady Lysander's very soul might be in peril. Could he save her from the vampyre's clutches, for he was in no doubt the ancient being belonged to that ilk of monster? Polidori and Le Fanu struck upon a theme in which to set their Gothic tales. He, on the other hand, must deal with the shocking reality.

Leaving the sunny dining room, the girls assisting Tabitha with household duties, the Rev Patrick Brontë caught sight of his son about to dash off, shouted from the study along the hall.

"Branwell, be a good fellow, fetch John Brown, will you? I am officiating at a funeral this afternoon at one, my offices required to chair a meeting of the Haworth Archaeological Society at half past three here at the parsonage. A grave must be dug, a pauper child by the name of Hogg passed away from consumption at Oakley House. His mother has been informed by my curate, the poor lamb."

"Pernicious anaemia, best treated with raw liver or hog's stomach," the doctor surmised while pausing to fill two vials from jars on the shelf before applying labels. "Taking into account the symptoms you describe, the fact that patients are only in the early stages of consumptive illness, I am left in no doubt that significant blood loss may be responsible for the drastically weakened condition of Mr Sidley. Additionally, this has brought about the death of Freddie Hogg the pauper child. Who though his constitution was by no means robust, his lungs inflamed, was, upon admission fairly strong and well nourished. I cannot, of course, comment upon the puncture wounds to the neck of patients. I am not the resident physician at the sanatorium. A Professor Philpot is in charge. But you know what you have been at great pains to explain, Branwell, ties in exactly with my own concerns regarding this Palaeolithic, whose dog-like fangs I saw for myself. A witness to the excavation of the carcass over at the standing stones. To my mind, a number of explanations are in order. Any palaeontologist must question why a body preserved in peat might be pinned down by iron rods. Surely of some significance that the prehistoric community must have sought fit to restrain one of their own in such a manner."

"Because Dr Otley, they understood what we now realise. He was a vampire. A creature of the night full of evil intent. Their village elders, if we may term them thus, acted partly through desperation, but they must also, far from resembling grunting, semi-ape-like primates, have possessed intelligence. Maybe even a knowledge of the spirit world, knowledge that we can learn from."

"Agreed," answered Otley, folding his arms. "Given the serious nature of this matter, it is imperative we stay balanced in our judgement, commit nothing rash or unconsidered. How do we deal with a dangerous creature capable of replicating a Lakeland poet and holding a civilised conversation? We must behave like gentlemen, maintaining the utmost respect for Lord Edmonton. Our next move, young Brontë, is to attend that meeting at half past three."

Branwell shook his head and sighed. "Be polite if you will, but for heaven's sake we must work fast. The daylight hours only. Dear God, what we might face when the sun is down, I dare not contemplate. The awful truth is that, like it or not, Lord Edmonton finds himself in league with this thing as its protector. The fellow surely knows a good deal more than he is letting on. That infernal carcass must be seized, impounded and destroyed by nightfall. Given another day, a week even, it's strength will grow. The requirement to feed. It may not only be the paupers who shall fulfil its dietary requirements."

"Quite, I take your point."

The funeral of the unfortunate Freddie Hogg took place at one o'clock as planned. The grave properly dug and filled in by the sexton. The coffin brought from the sanatorium, hardly cheap as befits a pauper, but constructed by the local joiner and cabinet maker. Expenses met by Lord Edmonton, the vicar applauding this act of selfless generosity.

Though poorly attended, being towards the end of the summer, birds sang sweetly from the church's guttering and wild flora grew abundantly about the kirkyard.

The weather sparkling and sunny. A solitary wreath, inscribed from Lord and Lady Edmonton, lay atop of the grave mound. Small memorials in sight of the church attested that many children died in infancy from typhus, cholera and tuberculosis.

The vicar performed another three funerals that week and comforted the bereaved.

Like the washing left out to dry, the burial of young Hogg caused no ripple of concern amongst the group of archaeologists visiting the parsonage that afternoon. The momentous discovery of a prehistoric man buried for millennia at the standing stones was foremost in their minds, when the front door to Glebe House was flung open in greeting by Rev Brontë. The chairperson to oversee the meeting.

The clergyman's ground-floor study hung with three notable biblical scenes by the engraver John Martins was commodious enough. To the right of the fireplace, his neat desk with a brass candlestick, snuff box and tobacco dish, together with his flintlock. To the left, the cabinet piano pressed against one wall, the vicar's walking cane leant against it.

For this afternoon's gathering a piano stool plus assorted hardback chairs were arranged for the visiting gentlemen in a square, around a colourfully weaved Kidderminster rug.

The congress of the H.A.S. committee proved both good-natured and well attended. Port passed round and pipes smoked agreeably.

The arrival of Dr Otley caused a brief interruption. The society's chairperson, after taking him aside, deemed it necessary to allow a short speech relating to a controversial development about the Palaeolithic man, that should tax the brains of the committee members, that some found hard to fathom.

"There can be only one thing for it," said an exasperated Rev

Brontë, having his meeting interrupted in such a dramatic fashion. "Dr Otley, Branwell, you must allow Mr Clarke, Frank Bishop, Sir Fenton, John Martin, Mr Clough and myself to accompany you over to Oakley House. There we may enquire *in a civilised way* the exact whereabouts of the peat man, and then demand to see the carcass so we may make up our own minds as to these charges levelled against His Lordship. For want of better words, 'harbouring a vampire dangerous to human life'. A thoroughly bad lot by the sound of it. I cannot be fairer, and I put this motion forward to the present committee."

"Seconded," said Sir Fenton, puffing on his clay churchwarden pipe, tobacco smoke rising ceiling-wards. "The three iron rods are contentious. Why should this prehistoric man be restrained in the first place - pinned down in such a grisly fashion? I grant you Dr Otley, call us amateurish, but in our impatience to have the remains exhumed, the team was perhaps rash to move the body without first consulting museum records of funerary rites, ancient pagan burial customs and ceremonies. I like the vicar, am of the view that the matter is serious and that it is our duty to act. What harm be there? It is our right, as fellow members of the H.A.S. to be privy to the preservation of the specimen. A request to view and record for ourselves the rate of decomposition will be perfectly acceptable, in no way at odds with our relationship to the society's patron. If there is nothing untoward, surely committee members will be granted immediate access to the library, or wherever the carcass is presently lodged. Amateurs we may be, yet the professors from York have not so far shared one jot of their findings, nor offered reports. I find that unacceptable. They are *the outsiders* and he is *our* discovery, after all."

A round of applause followed.

"Hear, hear. Bravo. I believe the motion carried," agreed Mr Clarke, snatching his hat and cane ready to leave. "What say you, Frank Bishop?"

"Of a like mind. Lord Edmonton must be brought to account," he added seriously. "Carriages await along Church Street. To Oakley House this instant!"

***

Lord Edmonton was soon forced, by sheer weight of argument to reveal the exact state of preservation. The present condition of the body laid out on straw inside a packing crate, balanced on trestles in the library.

To the utter shock of those present, it must be reported that the state of preservation confounded natural laws and those of science also. The expected decomposition of tissue was nowhere in evidence. Instead, a reversal had taken place. The facial features pink and rosy-cheeked, showed every aspect of youthful vigour. The flesh now supple and well nourished, hair and beard shiny, bristling with vitality.

Despite opposition from the professors (Harman, Cobbs and Philpot), pathetic protests that mere water treatment be responsible, the cadaver rehydrated, not in the slightest extraordinary.

Sir Fenton, showing admirable restraint given the ghastly evidence provided, ordered that the carcass be passed into the jurisdiction of the committee and in due haste, returned to the site of the standing stones for reburial.

Faced by the sheer volume of the determined officers, the cleric, Branwell, Dr Otley and even the Lady Lysander, Lord Edmonton had little choice but to comply. The crate nailed up, taken back downstairs to a waiting carriage and strapped with due care to the roof in preparation for a return journey to the ancient megalithic site up on the hill.

Being summer it would remain daylight till nine.

It was said that at the very time, around twilight, the carcass of the prehistoric fugitive was being reintroduced to the acidic ground at the standing stones, with precautions. The reintroduction of the iron rods hammered home in the same exact positions upon the body as before. At Glebe House, some miles distant, Emily was upstairs in her room busy lace making. Her pillow on a stool in front of her. Her design for a place mat laid flat, bobbins and pins in position. Happening to glance up from her work to see in the fading light of eventide the crimson-eyed child, Freddie Hogg. Liberated from the clay, sprung from the churchyard. His face a rotted yellow, tapping, or rather scratching, with talons at the window, begging to be allowed in. This was two storeys up, without visible assistance from either a ladder or the bough of a tree. Red, glowing pupils beseeched Miss Brontë to comply with his dearest wish to be allowed entry.

Wisely Emily did not attempt to raise the window, for she saw quite clearly the teetering smile upon young Hogg's blackened lips, revealing a pair of pearlescent fangs.

As the clang of Sir Fenton's hammer struck home the last of the iron rods, at that same moment in time, the form of the monstrous child hovering at the window disintegrated. Sent forth to his proper dominion - to disturb the living no longer.

Thirty One

A fortnight after the reinterment at the standing stones, the prehistoric fugitive laid to rest on the moors. Dr Otley found himself, upon a stormy night with drains overflowing, called out on a curious mission.

His stalwart nag was ascending, following another horse slowly clopping to the summit of Main Street to the little square of shops and public houses.

The doctor had been staying in Haworth with his father-in-law, the architect.

Thus, being the nearest available physician, got knocked up by a thoroughly drenched Justice of the Peace called Mr Merrill. Both men dismounted and tethered their horses between Thomas and Sons, the wine merchants, and The Cross Inn - one closed at that hour, the other thriving and boisterous.

Parked in a largely deserted area on the gleaming cobblestones, was a horseless carriage, the lamps either side of the box seat aglow. A large, bracketed street lantern set into the wall above highlighted its abandonment. Mr Merrill, a tall gangly gentleman of some means, gave Otley a nod. Plucking one of the lighted carriage lamps out of its slot, the doctor opened the door of the carriage, peering into the interior. Sprawled upon a plush, velvet seat, was a naked wild-haired young man. Clearly the victim of a fatal violence, although there was hardly any mark upon the body to talk of.

"Blazes, Otley, I've no idea who he is."

Leaning forward through the open door, the doctor adjusted the light revealing a pleasant, undisturbed face. Taking professional account, the blood had been drained, the smooth skin resembling porcelain. Keeping his nerve, a miniscule wound was evident upon the victim's chest – a patch of coagulated crimson.

"Stabbed through the heart, death instantaneous. You'll observe Mr Merrill, not much blood evident to the front, perhaps the greater effusion will appear when I shift it round. As you can see, we merely have the entry wound, a small trace of blood, the back of the body remains unblemished. Internal bleeding perhaps? I tell you what," he suggested, rain dashing from his wide-brimmed hat. "There is a fellow maybe able to deduce something of this. Excuse me Merrill, while I go and fetch him from the snug at the Black Bull."

"Whoever's that?" asked the other.

"Branwell Brontë."

"The curate's son. Hmm, yes, I read one of his political poems in the *Halifax Guardian*. Wasn't there a matter of stolen monies while working as a booking clerk? Inclined to rowdy company, drink and opium – spared the court so far, but only just mind." Merrill quickly changed tack. "And to think our abandoned carriage might have remained uninvestigated for some time yet, had not Barraclough the clock maker been walking past and tripped on a paving slab, grabbing the door handle." He ably demonstrated the point. "Happened to catch a glimpse through the window of this young man. I mean, for public decency's sake, we must get the four-wheeler removed. I've sent an urgent request by messenger. I await the arrival of officers from Bradford. My dear chap, I've become a drowned rat. Get a move on, collect your charge."

Branwell was fortunately not yet fully inebriated. Sat in his favourite chair regaling his friends with amusing anecdotes. Nursing a brandy fireball, he greeted Dr Otley heartily. Whispered words were exchanged, enough information to allow the red haired, bespectacled young poet to leap up and forthwith accompany the respected physician outside and into the rain.

"Murder, you say," young Brontë sloshed his way through the puddles. "By God Otley, that's the carriage is it? Can't say I recall seeing that four-wheeler outside the Cross Inn when I came down the church steps earlier."

"Time?"

"Around twenty-five past seven. How was murder done, if I may be so bold?"

"It's all conjecture at this point, but I'd hazard a long, sharp cloak pin," answered the physician, dreading his revealing the identity of the corpse. "Driven home with considerable force then hurriedly withdrawn. Not much blood to be seen. Look here dear chap, I'm so sorry to be the harbinger of dreadful news... but it's your friend Gordon Aboyne."

"Gordon, what, you're sure?" Branwell was laid dumb, shocked to the quick, but he managed to keep his composure. Another hour he reflected, would have likely seen him insensible, soaked with gin and brandy. The matter was serious. Mr Merrill, who he knew, was a Justice of the Peace and respected Lodge member like himself, a Freemason.

Branwell was attentive, willing to put his all into finding out who on earth would kill such a likeable fellow on the brink of artistic fame, his funerary sketches likely to be reproduced on glass lamp shades, curtaining, cushion covers and wallpaper - to be sold in mourning departments in large department stores from York to London.

Branwell assessed the pale, muscular torso. "I might begin by saying, Mr Aboyne's state of undress may not be taken as so surprising. Not necessarily taken as 'sensational'. We'd better deconstruct."

"Well, you do that for us," said the physician curtly.

Branwell's brow furrowed, his lips pursed before he spoke. "When I last greeted Gordon at the Black Bull, he reminded me it would soon be the full moon. This is of importance gentlemen, nothing mystical, merely akin to sea bathing at Yarmouth or Scarborough."

"Go on."

"He is, or rather was, a committed 'moon bather', a lunar relaxation referred to by De Quincey as wholly beneficial to the body. The moons radiance, full of vitamin particles and stellar neutrons unseen by human eye. The full moon, that natural satellite, fell exactly when, gentlemen?... last night. At that time of maximum rays the moon bather can absorb its full radiance."

"Moon bathing is entirely lost on me," exclaimed Mr Merrill, doubting the significance. "So De Quincey approves does he? A fine thing."

Holding back the tears the young Brontë prodded about dark corners, particularly the seat cushion, finding a scrap of crumpled paper. The writing barely legible, produced by a scratchy quill pen. This torn paper he deduced represented an invoice, or at least a portion of one.

"Pray, is discarded litter really of any value to this enquiry, Mr Brontë?" asked the magistrate's attendant with an air of pomposity.

"If it's a hired carriage, other occupants' debris possibly. Hard to tell at this point."

"Well, the note may hold a clue," said Otley, mindful of his tall hat, moving deftly out of the carriage back down onto the wet pavement where a small crowd was gathering. He supported Branwell's elbow, guiding him to avoid splashing into a deep puddle.

"Who then, was murdered? By God, not a stranger, yet one of my dearest acquaintances," pronounced young Brontë. "I very much wonder Mr Merrill, if I might retain this torn scrap of useless paper." About to place the grubby, crumbled-up invoice in his long pocket, he awaited final permission.

"I'm sorry for your loss sir, if you see something worthwhile in that chit keep it by all means. However, if the law officers from Bradford express interest, you must return it. Now of greater importance perhaps, whatever happened to the horse that drew the carriage up here Otley? I made enquiries to the publican who knows the stalls stabling arrangements, and he could not account for the animal's whereabouts."

"I think it most probable," replied the attendant physician wryly, "the driver of the carriage, or should that be more probably 'the murderer', would have employed the horse to make his escape. Either onto the high moors, else back down the hill and into the valley. Take your choice."

"More than one of 'em, perhaps," concluded Mr Merrill, replacing the lamp in its bracket, the wick smouldering woefully low. "On the night of the full moon. Moon bathing indeed. I am incredulous to the fads of young people."

Once the Bradford officers arrived to take charge, Dr Otley, able to share the modest results of his preliminary examination, felt intimidated by these stone-faced Yorkshire lawmen, more driven by far to meet up with Branwell the next day, thereby, with the advantage of the young man's ambidextrous mind, commit to certain enquiries and find out why Gordon Aboyne should be stabbed in such a sophisticated way, and by who.

Leading his horse back down the steep incline the good doctor was expectant of a large brandy and soda, a cigar and his father in law's company to purge the past couple of hours. To discuss with him the bizarre murder of a young artist, whose only obsession was not really that of death, but of using his pencil to illustrate the British way of cloaking its finality.

What should the Rev Patrick at Glebe House make of this black news, he wondered? Branwell he felt conducted himself very well considering the harrowing circumstance of his friend's sad demise.

In death, left abandoned on four wheels in a rainstorm.

The following morning, Dr Otley, not normally a curmudgeonly person, was to be found with his breakfast roll unfinished. Peering discontentedly out of the window at the tumble of cottages opposite, straining to see a familiar red-headed figure approach.

But Branwell had yet to show at the coffee shop, their prearranged meeting place. Given that young Brontë was not the most reliable, perhaps this state of affairs was to be expected.

Finally, exasperated, and unable to wait a minute longer, the physician paid and ventured out onto the street, gladdened to see, hurrying down past the butcher's the diminutive figure of not Branwell, but Charlotte, clinging onto her bonnet, skirt flying. A little out of breath, she was quick to make amends.

"Doctor," said she, "profuse apologies from my brother. He fell ill and is confined to bed. Papa insisted."

The treacherous weather of the previous night had long blown itself out, yet there remained above Haworth a blustery, overcast sky. The sharp wind and light shower caused the pair to duck into a shop porch. A plain, honest woman known for her northern bluntness; Miss Brontë got straight to the point.

"Branwell showed me the scrap of invoice, I recognised the writing." Miss Brontë carefully withdrew the fragment from her bag. "I felt sure from the first."

Trouble had been taken to smooth the paper with a heated iron.

"Admirable, I'm sure. But first Charlotte, might I enquire after your brother's health. I have a fine regard for him. Could you tell me, did he perhaps catch a chill in the square? I'll call on him later, you can depend upon it."

"Nothing would give me greater pleasure," she answered. "At breakfast Branwell ate heartily, he was fully affectionate towards his sisters, but us naturally wondering at the latest news of Gordon's death. He outlined with so much zeal the scene of the horror. The carriage interior, the nude state of the body with a single wound. He must have over-exerted himself for he took a sudden seizure, was revived and led upstairs by Papa."

"Heart palpitations, your father's sound sense prevails."

"Yet, let us be clear, Dr Otley, my brother's frail constitution, his inability to attend your appointment alters nothing. I sir, shall willingly step into the breach. After all my sisters and I were well acquainted with the cemetery artist. If I can even in a small way, bring this criminal to face justice, I would thank God for the opportunity."

"I fully concur a capital offence deserves as much."

"I cannot yet countenance that," she continued, "He, transported into spheres of Gothic glory, shall n'er more grace our parlour table sharing his books crammed full of funerary depictions. Swindled by cruel murder. I heard of a firm at Hebden Bridge keen to produce fabrics blocked to his patterns. Gordon last told us of lantern glass shades finely engraved with reproductions of his sketches."

"Indeed, now, to return to the scrap of invoice."

"Very well doctor," Charlotte replied. "The scratchy quill pen is habitual to Mr John Greenwood who owns a small grocers, that also serves as Haworth's bookshop. He generally goes out of his way to help customers."

"The little fellow. Yes, I know him. Sells cheap editions."

"The type of paper, the scrawl mostly illegible, is his. I possess an identical one for a set of books I purchased from his shop last month. The invoice taken from a pad."

"Then Miss Brontë, let us lose no time and enquire of that same bookseller to whom the note might have been issued. This seems a strong line of enquiry."

Mr Greenwood, of no.36 Main Street, one property down from Overdale Terrace, a stationer by trade, was emphatic. "According to my ledger it was for a set of books sold to a Mr Aboyne only last week. The gentlemen, such as yourself, Miss Brontë, a loyal customer of long-standing. He once showed me you know, a folder of his work. I felt privileged, praising his eye for detail. though not the subject so much. He wished me to place some of his mounted sketches in my shop window, for which I declined. Ah, consulting my ledger I see, corresponding to this tattered piece of invoice, which it is true I alone can decipher, one of the purchases was a vast calf-bound book, containing plentiful engravings titled *Sacrificial Standing Stones Existent in the British Isles - the links of such monuments to primitive religion* by Sir Leonard Fuller. Another, a slimmer volume of sixty-five pages *The Haworth Archaeology Society Monthly Journal – a report upon recent excavations* by R. Clough and Sir Fenton. How is Mr Aboyne, by the way? I trust his art prospers."

"Alas, Mr Greenwood, I regret to inform you that he was murdered in strange circumstances. More than that, I cannot say. There will follow a funeral announcement in the newspapers, I am sure."

"Gracious that's damnably bad." The trader, encumbered by a curvature of the spine, responsible for producing a hunched back appearance was genuinely saddened by the unexpected news.

Dr Otley raised his wide-brimmed hat allowing the diminutive Charlotte, in her bonnet and skirts, to whisk past before quitting the shop. The fact that Gordon sought authoritative writings on the standing stones, that same region where the creature was not only discovered but also hastily reinterred, concerned him.

Thirty Two

Branwell rolled over in the folds of his bed, the curtain tied back, the staircase clock had just chimed two of the morning.

Charlotte had earlier taken him a bowl of beef broth, giving him a full account of her visit to the bookseller.

Considering his impetuous nature Branwell had been wrestling for a time on a point of romance.

He considered the poor prospects of a habitual lounger wanting for a direction in life, an individual who despite mixing easily with the wealthy and the upper echelons of society, never really was able to embrace for his own the picture of loveliness living at the Worth Valley country seat of her husband Lord Edmonton.

Unbeknown to either Tabitha Aykroyd the servant, nor his ever-vigilant father, luck would favour the bold, for he only last week secreted a bottle of medicinal laudanum beneath his mattress. During this latest bout of illness, he found considerable relief in taking measured sips.

Lungs unburdened of catarrh, respiration improved for the last couple of hours, his thoughts drifted upon what might have been had he been born a gentleman of leisure, awash with a fortune. Then he would have won the heart of Lady Lysander from that awful Lord Edmonton. Who's accommodation of the prehistoric creature at his country house surely linked him with occultism and diabolical acts of necromancy.

One could dream of course, Branwell felt owed his due. Despite his moral failings he yearned that his poetry, yet to find recognition, might take off. With the masses willing to part with their cash. To rise amongst literary giants like Byron and Wordsworth, Southey, and Coleridge.

A gentleman poet, set to earn a fortune, allowed to indulge his every whim - now that was more like it!

Feeling chirpier, the young Brontë began to hum a catchy organ number composed by Bach, music which he himself enjoyed playing. A great favourite, oddly enough, of his deceased chum, the artist Gordon Aboyne.

Uncannily, the piano downstairs in his father's study, seemed to be jingling of its own accord, playing a worthy accompaniment, floating upstairs to the landing.

The candle beside his bed briefly flared. The figure of Gordon Aboyne stepped forward from the gloom, totally renewed like a Grecian statue.

"My dear old dog, you look well, death suits you," uttered Branwell, sitting up, well acquainted with hallucinatory states and not so easily ruffled.

"I assure you Branwell, I do not feel at my best. Far from it. I am in the primary stages of change and the agony is unrelenting, every nerve fibre, vein and artery stiffened on fire. I submit to you an undead state is not all it's cracked up to be. I have, you will see when my lips part, a long razor-sharp tusk developing central to the upper quadrant of my normal teeth. Fables claim that the canines are what develop, yet I have found that a single sharp protrusion is the means of supping upon prey. You will recall, perhaps, this small wound upon my chest caused, I can vouch, not by a blade or needle, but the same tooth type rendered by my attacker."

"Well. I shall decline offering you a drink Gordon. My life blood is precious to me for presumably, that is part of the reason why you chose to return, to sup on my veins. You tempt me, but I decline."

"Forgive me and allow me to explain myself. I was set upon at the standing stones, my memory grows so vague, it being difficult to remember exactly what did occur. I have some inkling - I trekked with my haversack to Ponden Clough, up by Crow Hill, the standing stones attained as dusk fell. I ate a little and drank from a flask of wine - deposited my clothes in a neat pile on the dark edges of heather-tufted turf some distance from the burial place. Both comfortable and in good spirits."

"Moon bathing, you are an enthusiast. We are clear upon that point. My sister Charlotte reliably informs me you purchased a quantity of books from John Greenwood upon the subject of the standing stones. The various volumes must have fired up your determination to visit the megalithic ruins on the night of the full moon."

"If you say so, but also *sketching by moonlight*, in my deteriorating state of humanity, the one boon I can at least offer is my notebook. I was able, before the attack, to hide it behind a small rock fringed with purple gorse. A crossed pencil and charcoal stick mark the place. If you can locate that sketchbook, you may be able to protect others. I suppose I am spared extinction in a public cemetery at least. Farewell, damn you."

"One moment," the white-fleshed nakedness of his friend showed a contrasting discrepancy. "Do you realise, Gordon that the back of your hands are scaly-skinned."

He barely cared. "Symptomatic of the reversal of rigor mortis I suppose - an aspect of transfiguration."

The task of retrieving this notebook from the prehistoric site was at that time quite beyond Branwell's physical capabilities. He was still far too weak.

However a short while later a solution beckoned, for not long after breakfast, Branwell's friend Enoch Thomas, the landlord of the Black Bull called in at the parsonage to visit the recovering invalid and finding him in tolerable health surreptitiously handed the young reprobate a pint of gin, disguised in a rolled cloth cap.

Mentioning he would be riding past the standing stones in a trap to visit a friend over at Lothesdale. Enoch promised to make a pause in the journey.

This he did. With a little searching around he located Gordon Aboyne's damp sketchbook behind a rock. The pages stuck fast due to the night-time moisture on the moor.

The notebook duly placed in his luncheon knapsack, more prizes followed. For Enoch recovered a small pile of gentleman's clothes further afield, a silver flask glinting in the prickly furze. The book hardly glimpsed over, on returning to Haworth that same evening,

Mr Thomas duly dropped the items off at the parsonage, wishing young Brontë a speedy recovery so that he might resume his favourite chair in the snug and resume his considerable intake of brandy. The publican left to take up his duties at the Bull.

The materials deemed fit for proper investigation Dr Otley was summoned, as was Mr Merrill on behalf of the Justice of the Peace.

Anne, Emily and Charlotte supervised tea, while the gentlemen gathered round the polished dining table. The Rev Brontë deeming it important enough to delay his parish work quitted his study. He smoked his clay churchwarden while Branwell stood at his side, still the invalid, wearing his slippers and gown. The magistrate's assistant Mr Merrill made a suggestion to which the clergyman complied – that the servant, Tabitha, after they had the opportunity of closely examining the murdered man's belongings, might wrap the loose garments, sketchbook and silver wine flask in brown paper secured with twine, for evidence to be passed on to the Bradford officers.

"May I be permitted to congratulate you Branwell, upon commissioning Enoch Thomas to secure these articles," said Mr Merrill, by way of an opening.

"The greatest pleasure," the young man did his best to explain, although remained guarded upon certain points. "The possibility struck me that Gordon might moon bathe at this location, an intuition, although I am told by Dr Otley he had recently wanted to learn more about the monoliths."

"Indeed."

"Mr Merrill?" asked Charlotte.

"Ma'am," the agent answered, putting down his teacup whilst she passed him a plate of freshly-baked biscuits.

"Burial places were to fascinate Mr Aboyne. He consigned his art mostly to the cemeteries and churchyards of Yorkshire."

"Quite. Rest assured, I have become lately aware of the considerable portfolio of funerary subjects he amassed. That distant area of the moors should appeal - I perfectly comprehend."

"Oh yet what a sad sad business this murder is," offered Rev Patrick. "His poor mother is devastated, quite lost. She is in my prayers often. So to, the elder sisters. The funeral is yet to be finalised. Sometime next week probably."

"There, there, Papa," said Anne. "Gordon led a short life but a productive one."

"Emily, my dear," the curate burst out, "do please fetch your portable writing desk from upstairs. This fragile sketchbook is so damp from being kept in the outdoors. You might lean Mr Aboyne's drawings against that excellent piece of furniture."

Last night's bizarre appearance of his recently stabbed friend Branwell decided, was not a matter for discussion. Neither with his father or Mr Merrill, both rational thinkers. Arisen undead is hardly a feasible topic for an enquiry of this nature.

The procedure of examining Mr Aboyne's belongings began. No bloodstains, nor signs of struggle. The flask was likewise handled with care though nothing useful gleaned. Next came the notebook. Due to exposure, the covers came detached, certain of the stitched pages stuck. But the volume was in good enough condition to be examined within.

The young ladies present were no mean talents themselves, adept with watercolours and pencil and ink for portraits, since childhood sketching the natural environment around their home. Like the person who turns the pages for a pianist's sheet music, Charlotte did the honours with the sketchbook. Stood by Mr Merrill's side before the pedestal table upon which rested Anne's little writing desk.

The first sketch portrayed an incoming flight of birds against moon bright clouds. Dashed off with Mr Aboyne's usual flair using charcoal and soft-leaded pencil. His thumb smudging the open sky above, shading-in to good effect. His skill at capturing a theme quickly was evident, the subject perfectly natural given the moorland setting.

"Please do turn the page," said Mr Merrill dourly.

Charlotte did so. In the next image, certain of the winged ensemble, the supposed flight of birds, were now down in the middle of the stone monoliths. They were not birds at all, yet creatures of an indeterminate species.

"I suppose these are mere make believe, born of an overactive imagination," Suggested the magistrate's representative. The thick, leathery, veined wings, the long talons, the overall reptilian appearance just too outlandish.

"I dare say they are, sir," agreed the clergyman, puffing on his pipe. "Gordon's scene is deeply Gothic, with a dash of paganism. It is a really first-rate image. Don't you think so, my dears? I'd even say his imagination was a match for your own."

Branwell swallowed hard, beads of sweat dotting his brow, an uneasy quiver in his stomach from the fear of what he knew was to follow.

Another section of paper proved impossible to separate, so the next page of the notebook to be considered was the ninth.

At this juncture, the artist must have been seen from his vantage in the bracken and granite, one of the winged beings had separated from the rest. Caught by the sweep of his pencil, advancing towards him, this creature, undoubtedly female, for Gordon had filled in details such as leathery, breasts (each bearing three nipples).

Branwell had a serious intake of breath, causing his father to twist round. His inner sense aware there was more to follow. Turning over the illustration showed this time the creature up close, for the space between 'it' and Gordon had been reduced considerably. Encased between enormous ear lobes, surrounding layers of scaly skin the reptilian head revealed a human face. How Mr Aboyne kept his nerve with his pencil God only knew. Most would have fled for their lives.

Staring keenly with a smile on her voluptuous lips, a tusk like protuberance poked from the mouth, this bow-legged reptilian, part born pterodactyl, sprouting leathery wings and ferocious talons.

Branwell shared a glance bearing serious concern with Dr Otley. The sisters revelled in a different sphere entirely, being each wholly ignorant that the series of drawings were in fact bravely executed by Gordon Aboyne... just before he was attacked by a vampire at that prehistoric site.

"Dearest Papa," cried Charlotte, stifling her giggles, "Does not the face of the creature, though a little cruelly contrived by our cartoonist, bear a strong resemblance to the Lady Lysander. There is a beauty amongst the grisliness."

"Well, my dear, it is really quite surprising," he admitted, nudging his spectacles. "A fine caricature, although whether Lady Lysander Edmonton herself would approve, I doubt that very much. I had no idea Gordon could conjure up such vivid imagery, reminiscent of mythology, not merely a copier of antiquities."

Fig 5

Epilogue

The worms of olde England be encouraged. The condemned possessed the demeanour of a true Yorkshire gent, but shame upon the rowdy spectators. The prison cart's arrival to the scaffold hailed by vile oaths, others openly fornicating amid the dung and refuse piles of the marketplace.

At the top of scaffold steps the condemned forwarded toward the dreadful plank. With a low, ingratiating bow, the Scarecrow Bride made an appearance as hangwoman, from what we declare, memorable for flinging herself off that church tower some years back., an animated, billowing kite no less. Hardly pretty, but functional and in possession of a horribly rotten mangelwurzel face, she sought to chatter away regardless of solemnity due her jaw filled with clacking nails for teeth – giving as good as any old harridan.

Branwell Brontë, having fulsomely repented, we can report, awaiting the awesome machinery of justice, was unmoved by her rant, in tolerable spirits as she adjusted the hemp rope around his neck, and without due anxiety when the hood was drawn over, himself being naked as the day he was born.

"A poem ... a poem," the crowd shouted. Alas, no prayers offered, too *late, far too late for the scarecrow, the nails in her mouth clacking together. Showing impatience, she gleefully slammed back the trap lever before time, and that gentleman of leisure, so beloved of taverns in Haworth was flung into eternity, to twist and tussle a full ten minutes before expiring. The kite bride, meanwhile, flew upwards into the sky – lost to the clouds.*

Newgate Calender

No hero was he of the Glass Town saga. Oh, that at this time he could resemble more the Duke of Zamorna - yet, here he was, quite insipid, hating his feebleness, the whole of undying love, his troth to the Lady Lysander shipwrecked, his fantasy courtship and marriage too painful to contemplate.

All on account of those drawings. Prescribed a further day of confinement, Branwell summoned to his room upstairs his sisters to put forward an urgent agenda. Although breathing with difficulty, weak from little sleep, the young fellow was not to be argued with.

The girls were persuaded, despite their convictions to listen, to offer a sympathetic ear.

"But Branwell," Charlotte, tried to draw him gently into the real world. "Violet herself visited the Lady Lysander only last Monday. The professor assured her she is in excellent health and sends her fond regards to you. They took tea together. Lord Edmonton even found time to show what looked like his face for five minutes - positively polite and affable he was. There, what do you say to that?"

"But not, dear sister, *after dusk*. That is when the great change occurs. Charlotte, promise me that you, Emily and Anne shall this day take it upon yourselves to pay court to the Lady Lysander. I have already written a long-detailed epistle to Dr Otley, putting forth my experience. The visitation of *a renewed Gordon*. My conclusions regarding the sketch book... Oh, how you laughed my sisters, but you would not if you were aware of the terrible truth."

"That the Lady Lysander, that beauty of the Worth Valley, and her upstanding husband are ..."

"And others, Charlotte. Gordon Aboyne amongst them."

"And others, are part pterodactyl? Winged, scaly abominations that sup on the blood of the living. Really, you go too far." said Anne.

"I grant you, rules governing the species are open to interpretation." Branwell choked into his handkerchief. "Nobody can be expert. Yet Gordon seemed to me, beyond boundaries. A fledgling of something rarely, if ever, encountered, that patiently awaits our destruction, but which itself must be destroyed as with any plague. I am comforted that Dr Otley will know that delay will be foolhardy. ACT- while I lay abed, too ill myself to respond. Sisters, I implore you to be my eyes and ears. For God's sake, do as I ask. Take in the minutest detail, note everything at Oakley House. I suspect something – linger and go outside in the park if necessary, peep through the shutters of the tubercular ward. Visit the ward to view the no doubt positive results of Lord Edmonton's work, the façade behind his unbridled charity to others. Promise me?"

"My darling brother," Charlotte took his hand in hers, "anything that might sooth this nonsense seething in your breast, that might convince you otherwise of Gordon's state. His coming to you *after being murdered* is nothing more than a half-awake dream. These inflamed imaginings, transforming these goodly, honest, Yorkshire people into monsters."

"Visit Her Ladyship," he gasped, slumping back on his pillows, totally spent. "Ride over there."

"We shall comply. John Brown's old dog cart will suffice." There was a hollow, hopeless ring to Emily's voice for like the rest, she secretly wondered if her brother should survive this latest absurd crisis - such a bombardment of the human spirit.

"The letter," he croaked, rolling his eyes. "Posted yesterday. He will know what to do. Dr Otley, my dear old friend, he will act for the best."

The girls wishing no longer to linger beside the sick bed of their brother, their ailing, foolish brother at that, retreated downstairs for a cup of tea, their own views of the Lady Lysander undiminished, for to them, her Ladyship's visits to the poor, her tireless support of the tubercular ward at Oakley House, were exemplary. She was no monster in their eyes.

About to quit the parsonage, they were soundly berated by a concerned parent. "Girls," speculated their exasperated father from the depths of his study. "You are surely not thinking of venturing onto the moors? My dears, there is a treacherous sharp wind at this time of season, the days grow cold. Cannot you find useful employment pursuing your literary endeavours by the fireside?"

———

Charles Atwell, a captain of horse, was visiting Dr Otley with his wife. The couple having ridden the mail coach from Scarborough, on the coast of the north sea, via Haworth to Scrivelsby Hall, the physician's wife's country seat, although Otley remained during much of the week at Haworth attending to his practice, he was able at weekends, to assist Violet in managing the estate, and with their third child expected counted his blessings.

Drawing his friend aside after a sumptuous dinner (over brandy and cigars whilst the ladies withdrew) sat either side of the hearth. The stone fireplace covered with manorial carvings, he proposed that night an exhilarating ride across the moors.

"Charles, I beseech you, enjoy your cigar. I now deliver a lecture which I fear will seem at first incredulous. Yet from what I have myself researched and experienced first hand, tonight we must, together, brazenly engage upon the complete and utter destruction of a manor house."

"Must we be so horribly energetic?" Joked the captain, who loved the whole notion.

"The inhabitants of whom, I fear, are blood cultists aligned to the cult of vampyrism. Mark you, no madmen from an asylum, patients undergoing an aberration of personality, but a genuinely infected couple, Lord Edmonton and his wife, capable of *transfiguration*. They be far too gone. No mediator on earth can cause a reversal to goodness."

"Vampyres? I confess, I have touched upon the subject only marginally, having read the works of Le Fanu. What full-blooded man can fail to be stirred by his bewitching novel - Camilla?"

"Quite, this is not fictional, but ultimately bound to affect those of us who abide in this region. I wrote you already about the queer prehistoric man did I not? Dug up at the standing stones and pinioned by iron poles."

"You did. I recall the instance. You swore blue murder that he was, in fact diabolical in origin. Allowed, encouraged even, by Lord Edmonton, an antiquarian necromancer, to be released for a time, only to wreak havoc, then hastily reinterred by a much humbled society."

"Their lineage is not hard to fathom. Certainly, the Palaeolithic in turn infected a willing supplicant. Lord Edmonton, the chairman of that same archaeological society, his Lordship, thence at some stage, his wife. Now is grown a nest, a hive... hence my promise of a full night's work."

"On a side issue Otley, may I enquire if their canines are set similar to, say, a jackal, or our domestic cat – prominent sharp fangs set either side of the mouth?"

"According to young Brontë, they possess a retractable tooth central to the upper quadrant. A tusk, he refers to it as. They have the wingspan and horned heads akin to prehistory."

"Fascinating."

"Not, I hasten to say, if Charles you are on the receiving end. I'd more say lethal." Dr Otley smiled broadly and sipped from his bulb glass of Napoleon brandy. "A faint prick mark, hardly noticeable. Gordon Aboyne, before his unseemly resurrection, was his own corpse. The Lady Lysander's handiwork!"

"This chappie Branwell, your local aspiring poet, has he mettle enough? Will he shore up our defences tonight and keep lookout? I surely hope so."

"He ails and is not a well man. No, we approach this dangerous task just the pair of us. Charles, are you game? I know how you relish a tussle."

"Ye Gad, sir try to stop me. With sabres and flintlocks! I doubt their effectiveness very much. How the devil do you intend to accomplish such a *grand annihilation*, given these creatures' allegiance? They will surely put up a stiff fight. I'd rate our odds a thousand to one against."

"Timing is everything here Captain." The doctor pulled luxuriously on his Dutch cigar, reclining further into his carved oak chair. He knew to accomplish this task of destroying these creatures that he must pull something out of the hat - and he had! "I shall do my best to explain. To begin with, we find modern mining practices come to our aid. The odds will thus be narrowed dramatically to evens."

"How so?"

"Last night Charles, I rode over to Nab Hill. One of my father-in-law's old friends Mr Barker, a fellow both honourable and dependable in business, lives upon the southern boundary of the chapelry. He has done very nicely and accrued a considerable fortune from local millstone brought down from the moors, to be processed into roof tiles. He owns three successful quarries around Haworth. It struck me a month or so back, Mr Barker, or rather his overseers, should be allowed access to powerful explosives, powder and so forth. I, naturally, perused this line and as a consequence, I am the proud beneficiary of a box of fuses, sticks of dynamite and a tub of powder. All harmlessly carried back here on my horse. Now these incendiaries are stored in the outhouse awaiting our retrieval."

"Checkmate! A first-rate strategy, yet it will be a damnably risky enterprise."

"Not after we've placed these explosives round the house. A final point Charles, not a word to our wives. Our policy is total secrecy. I shall inform Violet that we intend to ride over to Haworth to visit my father-in-law on the 'morrow."

"Done."

A little way along from the side gate, the girls took charge of the dog cart, drawn by an old horse left outside the school where (at the age of sixteen) Charlotte became its first superintendent.

Their close family friend, John Brown the sexton, a mason by trade who owned the cart, lived along Church Street, a stone's throw from the parsonage. The bonneted ladies threw themselves into the day's jaunt with gusto on behalf of Branwell, the black sheep of the family.

Enjoying the ride across Haworth moor exceedingly well, the upper Worth Valley distant. A nip to the air, the nag clopping along at an even pace between the rows of dry-stone wall, none could fail to be moved by the sweep of hills and dales at harvest time. The landscape dotted with fields and grazing wildlife, the heathland with its spread of purple gorse, granite crags and outcrops of strangely formed rocks an ever present inspiration to the Brontë sisters.

There was no dread of failure, for they regarded their errant brother's mad instructions futile, misinterpreting Gordon's last notebook. Losing a close friend to murder, not being able to come to terms with it.

On a brighter note this was a day out, a chance to catch up with ladies' chatter, to see once more the Lady Lysander. Nor were they inferior society, being suitably intelligent and well-read - novelists in the making.

Most of what their brother had said gone in one ear and out the other they attained Oakley House, the seat of the Edmonton's, at around noon. Having travelled the moors, the sisters were warmly invited for refreshment after their combined management of the carriage and Munster, a surly horse brought out of retirement from the field.

Her Ladyship was a woman who could do no wrong in the eyes of their father. Not only for her supportive stance upon aiding the plight of poor, impoverished mill workers, but additionally supporting his ongoing campaign for better quality drinking water and proper sewage drains in the town, derided by many a rich mill owner.

Polite conversation ensued, pleasantries exchanged, until mid-afternoon, when Charlotte alone remembered Branwell's request - the main purpose of their impromptu visit. Thus, she enquired if they might be shown the famous ward.

A trifle reserved in manner, Her Ladyship answered, delicately sipping her China tea. "You're venturing upon the tubercular ward should be intolerable. I must prohibit it. An outbreak of sickness, otherwise it should give me the greatest pleasure to honour your request Charlotte. To be sure an enjoyment for perhaps... another day. They are being fed a basin of gruel about now. My orderlies advised a ban for the foreseeable future."

"A ban," said Emily, raising her eyebrows.

"For want of delicacy in your behaviour, why do you choose to question what I have already told you. Really, come now, such impudence."

For the first time, a shadow passed across Her Ladyship's features, as though she suspected an ulterior motive was being percolated. How then, could she possibly know. Her mood from that moment changed. She became short tempered, it became clear the sisters were not welcome. This rebuff hurt, especially Anne, who had played that afternoon so nimbly, so deftly phrased Mozart's six variations in 'F'.

"That will not do. No indeed it will not," said Emily, the middle sister brusquely, first to comment upon the mood swing as they quit the imposing front portico entrance. "Why, then, was Her Ladyship so affected by mention of the tubercular ward? Her excuse perfectly feasible, but her sudden anger."

"Emily my love, she is hiding a conceit, drawing a veil over some wickedness." Charlotte was blunt and to the point. "Before setting off homewards I propose dear sisters, that we carry out what our brother asked us to do in the first place - namely, investigate that ward. We shall start by taking a peep through the shutters. No one is abroad in the park and if by chance we do meet a maid or groundsman, who amongst the servant class will be impertinent enough to question our intentions of visiting the box maze. Brrrr, it grows chilly as the evening draws in does it not?"

The girls moved swiftly round by the side of one wing where was situated a waterlogged veranda for patients, supporting a canvas awning. Large windows stretching the length of the house, closed to general view being securely shuttered.

Edging her dainty feet along the puddles Emily was first to observe that one of the hinged panels below was loose. The sisters discovered that by raising apart wooden slats a view of the ward could be obtained.

But what horrors...

Blood spilled copiously upon filthy, soiled bed linen - a full quota of patients were shackled to the iron bedsteads, the linoleum vile with excreta. The poor souls writhed about, muttering incoherently, staring from their beds in a peerless agony of fear whilst what? Gracious heavens, what? The orderly, supposedly a guardian imbued to protect, to administer, was now scaly-skinned, either side of the curved spine... a pair of folded, leathery wings.

Making its rounds from bed to bed, the choice for its delectation was a petrified female, by trade a wool comber.

A retractable tusk emerged from the nurses hellish mouth, the poor unfortunate's neck grasped by talons. Enough was seen.

Of all people, the Brontë sisters were perfectly suited for witnesses, being such acute observers of what, upon this occasion, should best be termed *obtuse nature* at its worst, a most unbeguiling form (this degradation posthumously omitted from their famous diary papers).

Keeping cool heads, wishing the groom and his erstwhile lad a 'good evening', for the light had begun to fade, turning out of the gates, Charlotte, loosely holding the reins, when the dog cart swayed dangerously after one of its wheels struck a pothole.

Stars were emerging, the outline of a crescent moon above Ponden Kirk, when they were assailed by a pair of masked horsemen, well wrapped up wearing wide-brimmed hats kept low. Weighed down by heavy saddlebags they were heading in the direction from which they had come. The girls first took them to be bandits.

"Greetings! We are not highwaymen. Please keep your purses and jewels," laughed the taller of the two, astride of his well-tempered mare, Juniper. His mellow voice clearly recognisable as that of Dr Otley. "Charlotte, forgive my brevity," he continued, "you young ladies appear out of sorts." He glanced at Captain Atwell, whose eyes, above the black mask, twinkled mischievously.

"Such a pleasant surprise. I regret to council you gentlemen bandits," answered Charlotte, holding the reins of the dog cart, "that all our brother was at pains to express this morning, which I am ashamed none of us believed, nor cared less for was true, his words we took to be rubbish, born of sudden bereavement. You received his urgent postal epistle, I trust, Doctor?"

"I did, and you may assure your brother, perused the contents with great interest."

"The sketchbook," said Emily, "reveals their nature exactly. Gordon in his last moments as a Christian, a human conscience being able to convey a credible likeness,"

"They might as well have visited from some distant cold planet. The like of their kind be hard to wrestle with in our own minds. We witnessed one of these scaly creatures for ourselves, with our own eyes!" expressed Anne.

"Most excellent, most entirely admirable," spoke up the captain of horse. "You are speaking to the converted. The doctor and I are presently here on a mission to obliterate Oakley House - with those creatures inside."

"For now, pray inform your brother, ailing though he is to buck up. Buck up his wits, for this very night the captain and I stand upon the brink of modern warfare. At dawn's first light I promise no trace of these wicked 'conversions' shall remain. I promise you young Brontë ladies, to eat my hat if this be not the case. I have stated it plainly thus."

Charlotte gave a wry smile. "I trust you will keep to your word, sir.

"Although you have the advantage of us, gentlemen, confess, are you not the teeniest bit afraid?" asked Anne. "You seem to me about to embark upon some light, frivolous sport at Oakley House - a game of Happy Families, or Draughts. Does not the violent nature of these *transfigurations* cause you to quake in your boots, sirs?"

"That should certainly be the case, Anne. But timing is our ally. Exact timing. For like our own human species, these pernicious beings must return from their prey seeking and *rest* awhile. Thus, in this period of dormancy, we shall strike hard and fatally. Go home I beg you ladies to your supper. On no account should your dearest papa know anything about this scheme. It should break his heart, for the Lady Lysander and Lord Edmonton, in their former life, were very dear to him. Leave what you observed today at Oakley House unsaid."

An appallingly loud beating of leathery wings alerted the party, causing them to raise their sights above Ponden Kirk, to the expanse of sky. Quite breath-taking to see, were five scaly heathens taking flight from the grounds of the mansion, in search of succour. Charlotte fancying whence they soared, whether it be Keighley with a population of fifteen thousand? Their own beloved Haworth? Or even as far afield as the great seats of cloth manufacture Bradford and Halifax, none dared to determine in that cold, still silence.

The body of the mother appeared incorrupt. At the opening of the breast a quantity of fresh extravased blood was found. The blood in the cavities of the heart was not coagulated but liquid. All the internal organs were sound. The old skin and nails fell off and exposed fresh ones.

A woman named Ena aged sixty. She had been buried ninety odd days before. But what struck Doctor Otley who had known her for many years, was that in life she had been a thin woman whereas now she was plump, and under the dissection light revealed a strange amount of fat. She had protested in her last illness that she was the victim of a vampire.

An eight-day old child, which had been ninety days in the earth, this also in the so-called vampire condition.

The son of a mill worker named Frederick; sixteen years old. The body had been interred nine weeks before. It was quite sound and in a vampire condition.

Also, another mill workers son, aged seventeen years, had lain in the earth eight weeks and four days. His body was in a vampire state.

The same may be said of a girl of ten, who had been laid in the earth two months before. She was sound and incorrupt and had fresh blood in her bosom.

Mrs Smith, sixty years old, who died six weeks before the investigation, much liquid blood in the breast and the stomach, and the whole body in a vampire condition.

After this visitation all the bodies that were in vampire condition were beheaded and then burnt.

www.ingramcontent.com/pod-product-compliance
Lightning Source LLC
Chambersburg PA
CBHW072054110526
44590CB00018B/3162